D0761592

"HANDLING THE HEARTBREAK OF MISCARRIAGE . . . is a story, vulnerable and personal, of miscarriage. But it is also a medical, factual presentation of the 'what' and 'why,' too. I've been here. I've walked this road. I find this book a helpful and healthful blend."

> Ann Kiemel Anderson
> Author and Speaker

"An intelligent response to the private agony over a baby who didn't make it to birth. In the three decades since my own lost babies I have never read a more thorough and sensitive treatment of this common, yet always unique, experience of desolation."

> Jeanne W. Hendricks
> Author and Speaker
> Howard & Jeanne Hendricks
> Ministries, Inc.

Handling the Heartbreak of Miscarriage

NANCY RUE

Here's Life Publishers

Published by
HERE'S LIFE PUBLISHERS, INC.
P. O. Box 1576
San Bernardino, CA 92402-1576

HLP Product No. 951566
© 1987, Nancy N. Rue
All rights reserved.
Printed in the United States of America

Library of Congress Cataloging-in-Publication Data
Rue, Nancy N.
    Handling the heartbreak of miscarriage.

    1. Miscarriage — Religious aspects — Christianity.
2. Miscarriage — Psychological aspects.   I. Title.
RG648.R83   1987   155.9'37   86-22775
ISBN 0-89840-129-1 (pbk.)

FOR MORE INFORMATION, WRITE:

L.I.F.E. — P.O. Box A399, Sydney South, NSW, Australia
Campus Crusade for Christ of Canada — Box 300, Vancouver, B.C. V6C 2X3, Canada
Campus Crusade for Christ — Pearl Assurance House, 4 Temple Row, Birmingham B2 5HG, England
Lay Institute for Evangelism — P.O. Box 8786, Auckland 3, New Zealand
Great Commission Movement of Nigeria — P.O. Box 500, Jos, Plateau State, Nigeria, West Africa
Campus Crusade for Christ — P.O. Box 240, Colombo Ct. P.O., Singapore 9117
Campus Crusade for Christ International — Arrowhead Springs, San Bernardino, California 92414, U.S.A.

For my family
Jim
Marijean
and of course
William Bradley

ACKNOWLEDGMENTS

My thanks to the many people who shared their talents with me as I wrote this book:

To Dr. James Breeden, who painstakingly picked his way through the chapters so that the medical information would be clear and correct.

To Christina Hom and the Sharing Parents of Sacramento who let me peek into their hearts and lives.

To all the support groups across the country who provided me with invaluable information and, of course, support.

To the many bereaved mothers and fathers who labored through my interviews and filled out questionnaires and poured out their hearts.

To Jim and Marijean who put up with countless order-in pizzas and mountains of unfolded laundry and three months worth of dust while I wrote.

May the Lord bless you all!

CONTENTS

PART FIVE
Where Do We Go From Here?

PART ONE

What Happened?

David begged him to spare the child, and went without food and lay all night before the Lord on the bare earth. The leaders of the nation pleaded with him to get up and eat with them, but he refused. Then, on the seventh day, the baby died.

2 Samuel 12:16-18 (TLB)

ONE

It's an Everyday Event — Why Write a Book on It?

Several years ago my baby died: the never-born little boy who lived inside me for four months, the son I was just beginning to love, whom I scolded for giving me heartburn and a bulging figure. He was the baby whose face I never saw, whose cry I never heard, whose warm little body I never held in my arms.

Though it's been a long time, I still remember the night I lost him — the way you remember a haunting movie. It was midnight, and the doctor at the hospital told me I was on the verge of a spontaneous abortion, a miscarriage. An hour later, I was rolled into an operating room and put to sleep. In fifteen minutes, the baby was gone.

Yet I recall even more vividly bolting upright in bed the next morning, trembling in the wake of a heart-wrenching nightmare.

In the dream, I delivered my baby. A mob of doctors and nurses showed him to me, but just as I reached out to touch his cheek, they snatched him from me, dropped him unceremoniously into a plastic bag and carried him away.

The cries of the infants across the hall brought me back to reality. It really was only a bad dream. Yet my own circumstances seemed just as unfair.

As I listened to the hopeful sounds of the newborns being carted to their mothers, I was deluged with conflicting feelings. Although now, years later, the pain is gone and I no longer feel angry or guilty or ashamed, I still remember how much it hurt. The memory is just as fresh today.

If I can remember the pain years later, I know that right now many of the 800,000 women who lost their babies to miscarriage during the past year are hurting at least three times as badly. Ten percent of the women who will become pregnant next year will involuntarily abort their babies before they're able to hold them in their arms, and those women will hurt, too.

INTENSE FEELINGS

Perhaps you're one of those would-have-been mothers, or maybe your life is closely linked to someone who is. You may be a husband, a relative, a friend, or a pastor or counselor. Chances are no one has told you that it's OK for you to hurt, that it's normal if you feel anger and guilt. And grief.

Nobody told me. I heard comments like, "Well, Nancy, you know it's for the best," and, "At least you have a child already," so it can't be so bad," and, "He probably would have been deformed or retarded. You wouldn't have wanted that, would you?"

I flipped through my memories of friends who had "lost" babies, and there were plenty of them. But on my mental Memorex, none of the miscarriage patients I knew seemed to have experienced the agony I was going through.

Suzanne, a close college friend, miscarried in her third month, but she hadn't seemed too disappointed.

Ann, another college girl friend, lost a baby sixteen weeks into her pregnancy. It didn't seem to cause so much as a ripple in her life.

Even Lynda, a girl I'd taught with in the East and one of the most high-strung women I'd ever known, carried off her miscarriage with apparent ease.

I suppose I had developed a nonchalant attitude toward the issue, the way many of us downplay the possibility of ever suffering in an automobile accident. *A thing like that would never happen to me*, I thought. I never would have dreamed it could hurt so much. Everyone else seemed to shrug it off like they'd dismiss a sale they missed at Macy's.

But I found out it *can* hurt. Unlike Suzanne and Ann and Lynda, I couldn't be blasé. I'd never known such an onslaught of strong feelings, each tearing at me in its own agonizing way.

There was a sense of shame. I felt unfeminine because of my inability to carry out the most natural process a woman can perform. *Everybody* has babies. I had produced one myself two years before without so much as an aspirin. Now I obviously must be completely inept.

There was guilt. I must have done something wrong to make the baby die, even though I was so careful. I'd become pregnant while using an IUD (intrauterine device), and I wrestled with the possibility that it might have caused the death, that unwittingly I'd murdered my own baby. Worse still, the pregnancy had been unexpected. At first I'd been confused at the prospect of having another baby. I agonized over whether God was punishing me for not being overjoyed at the gift He was giving me.

I was afraid, too. Maybe something was terribly wrong with me. Perhaps I would never carry another baby to term, or perhaps never conceive again. I might even be emotionally disturbed, carrying on like this. Everyone else seemed able to cope with the tragedy with such aplomb when it happened to them.

Over it all lay a blanket of sadness. I didn't want those "other" children, "another" baby. I wanted that one, the son we were going to name William Bradley Rue. In spite of my mixed feelings when I first learned I was pregnant, I loved him. I had dared to picture what it would be like: carting him to the library while I did research, seeing his face light up when he saw his big sister, Marijean, rush out of preschool to meet us. He had become a part of my every waking moment in that way only a woman with child can know. Now he wasn't there any more, and I missed him terribly.

Jim, my husband, took me home from the hospital that morning, and I spent the next few days trying to keep the tears under control. The only thing that helped was talking, so I called every friend and family member I could think of and told the story over and over. They all listened attentively and sympathetically, but no one knew quite what to say.

At that time, I was teaching adult education classes in Reno, sixty miles from our home in Dayton, Nevada. I felt fine physically in a few days, and because I was afraid I would dissolve into a puddle of self-pity if I stayed home, I went back to work.

Snow had been falling for weeks, and one morning as I drove to school through stark white Washoe Valley, an overwhelming emptiness set in. The desolate winter seemed to stretch on forever, and so did my sense of loss. I was alone at last, and a conversation with God started — through a torrent of rage.

"Why?" I said out loud. "You know me! You knew I wanted that baby! Why did You let this happen? It isn't fair!" Driving almost blindly over the icy road, I let out all the anger I felt toward the doctors who couldn't help me, toward all those mothers on the ward who were probably taking their warm bundles home from the hospital that day, and toward my husband, who didn't seem to care about the loss of his son the way I did.

Most of all, I was incensed at God, who had always rewarded me for living a good life. What had I, or my baby son, done to deserve that kind of treatment?

I stayed angry for a while, though I'm sure none of the people who lived with me during that time would testify to that, because I used up most of my energy concealing my rage.

I only cried while driving to and from work. The rest of the time I dammed up the flood of tears, but an ever-present ache burned in my chest. I taught pronoun cases, attended faculty meetings, and put pigtails in my daughter's hair, all with a smile that felt painted on. As soon as I was alone, the courage I thought I was supposed to show slumped into a heap.

I suppose I would have fed on that fury until it pushed the rest of my feelings into an unreachable pit if it hadn't been for God who, in His unfathomable way, does make everything turn out all right. He hits us over the head, if necessary, to try to make us see things His way!

God got my attention for the first time about a week after my miscarriage. As I drove through the valley to work, I saw a solitary, fat hawk perched majestically on a power line beside the highway. I whipped past him, but his image stayed with me.

He sat straight and tall on the wire, puffed up against the cold, his beak engraved in the background of a listless sky. Everything around him said, "Give it up. Go hide someplace." But proudly, stubbornly, he preferred to weather it. He could stand up to whatever winter dealt him, as if he possessed some secret that had escaped the rest of the birds. *That hawk has guts*, I thought. *He isn't going to let the barrenness beat him, and neither*, I realized, *am I.*

"All right, God," I said, shaking a mental fist. "I hate this. I hate it that You took my baby from me. I hate it that I feel like I've been kicked in the stomach. But I'm not going to let it beat me. I'm going to find out why I feel this way, and I'm going to do something about it."

Then I added timidly, "But I can only do it if You help me."

THE SEARCH FOR ANSWERS

During the next few months, finding out *why* became my quest. I spent hundreds of hours poring over medical books and journals, reading countless volumes on grief, and interviewing doctors, nurses, counselors, clergymen and people who had experienced loss.

I discovered that I wasn't alone in my anguish over losing a baby. Just a few weeks after my miscarriage, Wanda, a co-worker I barely knew, sent me a note. "I lost two babies twenty years ago," she wrote. "I know how it feels. Call me if you need me." I did, and Wanda shared with me all the sorrow, shame, guilt and anger she'd felt so long ago.

Shortly thereafter, I went to California to spend a weekend with my in-laws. My mother-in-law was wonderfully perceptive. "I lost one between Jim and Brad," she said. "I'll always count that one as a child." Then she described the evolving stages of grief she experienced when her son Brad died at age nineteen. My reactions, on a smaller scale, were all those she described.

It occurred to me then that I could contact other women I knew who'd suffered from miscarriage — Suzanne and Ann and Lynda and more. Once the word was out that I was studying the subject, friends, acquaintances and strangers emerged with stories of their own. And not one — not even Suzanne or Ann or Lynda — said she breezed through it unscathed.

"I was afraid you'd think I was nutso if I told you how I was really feeling," Suzanne told me when I called her long distance. "I kind of thought so myself at the time!"

Ann and Lynda had similar confessions, and I realized that I'd reacted exactly as they had. I'd covered up my anger and tried to hold back the tears, while friends had assumed I was doing great.

I discovered that miscarriage is almost always accompanied by real emotional pain. A study done by Sara Wheeler and Rana Limbo, two registered nurses at LaCrosse Lutheran Hospital in LaCrosse, Wisconsin, showed that 75 percent of the women interviewed said they considered their miscarriages to be the loss of a *baby* and they experienced real grief.[1] Unfortunately, although most women think like I did, that they have no right to feel as downright awful as they do, the pain just doesn't go away unless questions are answered and feelings are dealt with. I know.

Slowly my anger and my guilt did go away, but the sadness lingered much longer than I thought it should have. I didn't go to God this time, though, nor did I turn to my husband or my friends or my minister. I decided it was time I handled it on my own. *Get on with life and forget about it*, I thought.

That wasn't the answer. As you will see, I continued to suffer needlessly because I didn't know how to handle my grief.

Nearly two years later, God dealt with me again, and I finally faced my grief and my need to deal with it rather than run from it.

Then I learned what it is to suffer from one of life's blows. *Then* I discovered what it means to "go to God" when life gets to be too much. Only *then* was I able to accept the words of a rotund, bewhiskered clergyman who wrapped me in a hug one Sunday morning and said, "Remember, that little baby is now cradled in the arms of a loving God. You can let go." Only *then* was I able to put my grief to bed.

I'm not sure when I made the decision to write a book about miscarriage from a Christian point of view.

Perhaps it was when I closed the second secular book on the subject and still felt dissatisfied. They both gave excellent information on the physical and medical — even the emotional and psychological — aspects of miscarriage, but neither of them touched on the burning theme that singed the edges of *my* questions: Where did our Lord fit into a tragedy like this? How and why did He allow it to happen? What did He do with my baby's soul? How could my faith help me through the loss of a dream? How could I come out of my loss being something more, something better?

Or maybe I decided to write this book when Sue, a beautiful, majestic woman of seventy years, called tearfully to cancel an interview I scheduled with her. She lost four babies to miscarriage forty years earlier, and she decided she couldn't talk about it. "I don't want to revive that terrible time," she said. Her voice betrayed the agony she'd felt in the distant past.

She'd never had her questions answered. She wasn't at peace.

I didn't want to continue to suffer in silence for forty years, and I didn't want any other woman to have to suffer either. The idea that writing a book might help began to take hold.

The urge to write became irresistible when I realized what suffering a miscarriage had done for me. Not *to* me, but *for* me.

As I look back to 1982 and picture myself then, I see a very different Nancy. Today's Nancy is wiser, certainly stronger, and more aware of what she can do, and definitely more committed in her walk with our Lord because of what she had to go through.

Most important, this Nancy is more compassionate than she once was and is infinitely more capable of ministering to people who are dealing with a loss of any kind. I feel driven to help people when they hurt, offering them the help our Lord gives.

Certainly other events have occurred in my life since then that have shaped the growing me. Knowing grief — and making every mistake possible in handling it — probably has done more to foster my spiritual growth than anything else.

I want that feeling for Suzanne and Ann and Lynda and Wanda and Sue, and for each of the 800,000 women a year who loses her baby through miscarriage. I also want it for their families and friends who will be so desperately needed to give comfort.

If one of those people is you, in this book you'll find the answers I've discovered to the questions that plague folks affected by miscarriage.

"What happened?" they ask. "Why did it happen? How can we deal with it? Are we alone? Where do we go from here?"

The answers come from my research and the counsel I sought. They also come from my own heart, where God Himself provided peace. I hope many of the answers God gave me will put your mind at rest, too. I've addressed the issues most families experience when they go through a miscarriage.

Yet every family is exquisitely different. Not everyone is affected by a miscarriage in the same way. If you view yours as simply a life experience, don't feel bad that your grief isn't as strong as mine or those of some of the other women you'll read about here. As Sara Wheeler and Rana Limbo pointed out, "Feelings are not right or wrong. They just are."[2]

But because much of what I say in this book is set against the backdrop of my circumstances, I'll begin by telling you what happened to me. I hope it will help you get past the first hurdle: knowing you are not alone.

TWO

When It
Happened to Me

I love the prophets in the Bible. If I'd lived in Old Testament times, I'd have hung around their tents, listening to their every word, and believing it all.

But if in September 1981 some bearded wise man had prophesied that in a few months I'd find myself pregnant with my second child, I'd have told him to go back and recheck his vision.

The thought of having another baby couldn't have been more remote. Life in the Rue household had just begun to settle into normalcy. After ten years in the Navy, my husband, Jim, had had a difficult time finding what civilian life offered that would satisfy him. Jim has twinkling eyes and a boyish smile, but he's an intense man with a strong sense of integrity and a need to get life's best. Just any job that pays the bills won't do for him. There had been a number of those, and only in the few months before that September had he started to find some satisfaction. To be responsible for another life wasn't on the Rues' wish list just then.

My career path had been rocky, too. I'd quit teaching high school English a year and a half earlier to pursue free-lance writing full time. I loved it, but I wasn't earning a living at it yet.

So I was back teaching again, part time. Although I worked only four days a week, traveling sixty miles each way kept me worn out and there was little time or energy left for writing. I co-authored a book and sold several short stories to magazines, but my secret dream of "making it" as a writer was constantly on my mind. Another baby would render that dream economically impossible.

Our daughter, Marijean, was the main reason we hadn't planned on having another child for a while. At age two, she was strong-willed and independent and kept my maternal wheels in constant motion. I was already struggling with the fact that I had so little time to spend with her, and the thought of adding another young'un would have been almost overwhelming.

So in September 1981, I was wearing an IUD and feeling secure in our plans for the future.

SURPRISE!

When I started to feel the familiar symptoms of pregnancy about November 1, I started making excuses. Probably I was sleeping so much because the 120-mile daily commute was taking its toll. Probably I was eating my brown-bag lunch during the 10 o'clock break and then going out for a double burger, large order of fries and chocolate shake at noon because my metabolism was changing at age thirty. Probably my breasts ached because it was time for my menstrual period to start. In fact, when I thought about it, I realized my period was . . . a month overdue!

When I missed my second period, Jim looked at my blossoming shape and said, "You'd better go see the Doc."

"The Doc" was Dr. Jim Breeden, head of obstetrics at Carson-Tahoe Hospital in Carson City, Nevada. Bringing Marijean into the world with his help had been such a positive experience, we'd developed a rapport with him that snapped back into place whenever I went in for an appointment.

When I called his office, his nurse urged me to come in right away. The urgency in her voice started a wisp of anxiety within me.

"If you *are* pregnant, that IUD has to come out right away, or you could run into some real trouble," she said.

But Dr. Breeden was cheerful when a cursory examination revealed that Baby Rue #2 was indeed well on his way.

"You're eight weeks pregnant," he said. "Were you ready for another one?"

"Looks like I don't have much choice," I said. I felt numb,

but his happy banter carried me through the initial shock.

"I don't look forward to everybody's delivery," he said, grinning as he jotted down June 7 on his calendar. "But we all had such a good time last time, I know I'm going to enjoy this!"

My insides whirled like a kaleidoscope. One flick of the wrist and I shifted from anxious expectancy to irritated disbelief and back again. But an irresistible love for the new life flowering within me began at once.

PRECAUTIONARY WARNING

"I want you to be on the lookout," Dr. Breeden said. "The IUD increases your chances of having a miscarriage over the average. You'll probably bleed a little just from having it out, but if you start to bleed heavily and feel pain in the midline," he stroked a finger up the center of his abdomen, "give me a call, and we'll get you into the emergency room."

"I'm just going to have to convert the garage into a family room," Jim said when I told him the news. "Then the baby can have your study for a bedroom and you can move your desk into the living room."

An image of writing the Great American Novel with a baby crawling between my feet and Marijean yakking nonstop flickered in my mind. It wasn't what I'd planned, but it wasn't too bad, really.

"What about your job?" Jim was asking. "What about some of the night positions? You could stay with the kids all day and then drive into town in the evening, bring the kids to me, and I could get them home and put them to bed."

Then I would work six hours into the night. That was a depressing thought. We looked at each other bleakly.

That night the bleeding started. At first it was just the spotting Dr. Breeden predicted. By the next morning, it had almost stopped. I kept telling myself that everything was going to be fine. The next night, however, the bleeding started again, heavily this time. There was no pain, but still I panicked.

We were spending the weekend with Jim's sister, Robin, and her family. I knew that several years before Robin also had become pregnant while using an IUD. She'd lost her baby shortly before the fifth month. Robin had lived two thousand miles from us then, so I heard very little about her experience. Now, as she tucked me into bed, I wanted every detail.

She told me about it matter-of-factly.

"There are two ways of looking at it," she said after she finished. "You can stay in bed and hope and pray the baby makes it, or you can go on with life as usual and, if you miscarry, you'll know it was just meant to be."

I know now that she was trying very hard to cover the memory of her own anguish. Then it seemed I must be an emotional weakling not to be so accepting of whatever would happen. I didn't know what to think or how to feel, and everyone seemed to be telling me I should do neither.

On the night we returned to Dayton, it became obvious that the bleeding wasn't going to stop again. I lay awake until morning, waiting for the pain to start, but praying it wouldn't.

As soon as Dr. Breeden's office opened, I called and explained the situation to a nurse I'd never met.

"Go on with business as usual," she said crisply. "He isn't going to do anything to try to save the baby at this early date. And call us if you have pain or if the bleeding increases."

I fully expected her to say, "Next?" I hung up the phone feeling worse than ever.

"Business as usual" was a joke. For the next few days I went to work, made casseroles and read Dr. Seuss books to Marijean. But all I thought about was the baby and what might happen to him. I hadn't asked for him, but I loved him, and I clung to hope as the bleeding slowed to a trickle and stopped. A few days later, though, I woke up in a pool of blood, and my hope disappeared.

No one at Carson-Tahoe Hospital seemed terribly concerned about my condition. The receptionist in the emergency room looked at me suspiciously and asked if I was sure I was pregnant. The nurse who ushered Jim and me into a curtained cubicle wore a starched face and curtly told me to strip down and slip into a hospital gown.

"I think I'm having a miscarriage," I said bravely.

She smiled a practiced smile. "Well, if you are, you'll live through it. Millions of other women have."

Lord, give me grace, I thought.

Jim took my cold hand in his two warm, paw-like ones. "Whatever happens, you know you can handle it," he said. "No matter what, it's going to be all right."

I knew he was only trying to help, but I'd heard about as much of that as I could take. Everyone seemed bent on assuring me that having a miscarriage would be no big thing, and I wasn't buying it.

"If I lose the baby, I think I'll have a right to be upset," I said.

"Well, sure. But it won't be the end of the world. You'll be OK."

Dr. Breeden arrived and examined me, and his diagnosis

restored my spirits a little. "You're still pregnant, Nancy," he said. "Your uterus feels about nine weeks along, and you haven't started to dilate, so that's a positive sign. But the bleeding isn't good. Let's do a sonogram."

A sonogram projects an image on a screen by bouncing sound waves through the abdomen in much the same way that radar locates a submarine. It revealed that perhaps I wouldn't have a miscarriage after all.

We saw that Baby Rue #2 was very much alive and fluttering around like a tadpole. I waved to him on the screen.

However, a large, dark blob in the placenta showed that I'd suffered a placental abruption, a partial tearing of the placenta from the uterus lining. Now, though, the placenta, which nourishes the baby during pregnancy, appeared to be in the process of reattaching itself.

"This looks good," Dr. Breeden told us. "Since everything indicates that the baby is OK, let's have you stay off your feet for a week and give this thing time to heal. Come back then, and we'll have another look."

It has always amazed me that points of confusion can merge in a single moment, and you hear yourself say, "Why didn't I see it that way before?" At that moment, the idea of being pregnant, of having another baby, of being a family of four — career or no career, money or no money — was good. I wanted Baby Rue to make it.

But the week that followed was wretched. Although there was no more bleeding and no pain, the waiting and worrying were torture. I watched soap operas until my eyes felt like laser beams, and I talked on the phone interminably. I wrote voraciously. I'm not sure how, because I couldn't concentrate, but I cranked out four short stories for teenagers that week. Each one surged with a kind of understanding and compassion for the plights of kids that I'd tried for in other stories but could never get on paper. I hurt, and no one seemed able to identify or understand why I felt so bad. *That must be how it feels to be a teenager,* I decided. Already I was learning to minister through personal crisis.

I also talked constantly to God, begging Him to let the baby be OK and give this story a fairy-tale ending. From a pregnant woman who wasn't sure what she wanted, I'd become a mother who thought she probably couldn't handle it if her baby died.

When finally the day of my next appointment came, it brought good news. Everything looked great in Baby Rue's world.

"I think you two are going to make it!" Dr. Breeden told me. "I'll see you in three weeks for your regular checkup. Take your vitamins and drink your milk . . ."

I'd have consumed a pound of thumb tacks if he'd told me to!

When it came time for my next checkup, Jim, Marijean and I went to the doctor's office together. Marijean sat on Jim's lap, her chocolate-fudge eyes wide with wonder, while Dr. Breeden checked out the size of my uterus and searched for the baby's heartbeat. As he listened his face flickered into a grin, and he handed the stethoscope to me. There it was: the familiar sound of a mop sloshing up and down in a bucket. "Hey," I said tearfully, "there's really a baby in there, and he's alive!"

Never had I felt that we were so much a family as when Jim and "M.J." scrambled up to the table and took turns listening to the newest member. "Thanks, Lord," I said as I watched their entranced faces.

The next month slipped by on the silk of anticipation as we planned for the holidays and for Baby Rue's arrival. At last I felt normal, physically and mentally.

THE GRIM TRUTH

At dinner one night when I was four months pregnant, I consumed more of Jim's spaghetti than he and Marijean put together. After tucking M.J. into bed, I retired with a book to a bathtub of hot water and bubbles.

Nothing could have stabbed me to the core more sharply than the sudden cramp in my lower abdomen and the sight of that tub filling up with blood.

I screamed for Jim who, in his confusion, irrationally tested to see how hot the water was. Then he tore for the phone. Numb, I climbed out of the tub, wrapped in all the towels I could find, and crawled into bed. *If I can just stay here for a while*, I thought, *everything will be all right.*

Dr. Breeden wasn't on call, but Jim talked to his partner, Dr. Myer. He questioned Jim thoroughly about the history of the pregnancy and told him to bring me in to the hospital. Jim explained that after the recent snow our roads were icy, but the doctor said firmly, "Try to make it." Neither of us liked the sound of that.

We didn't say a word on the way. Jim concentrated on driving, and I on praying. I couldn't think of anything to say to God except, "Please!"

They were ready for us at Carson-Tahoe this time. A cute,

elfin nurse led us to a cubicle, chatting lightly. I couldn't focus on what she said, but she didn't assure me I could "handle it," and for that I was grateful.

"It always takes me awhile," she said cheerfully as she moved a prenatal stethoscope over my abdomen. "Nine times out of ten I can't find the heartbeat at all, and then the doctor comes in and picks up on it right away."

"He had a hard time finding it last time," I said weakly. Jim just pursed his lips and squeezed my hand.

Dr. Myer arrived shortly, snow still tipping his hair. He was young, with an upbeat personality, but the concerned set of his jaw scared me.

He, too, hunted for the sound of Baby Rue's heart and grimly did an internal examination. In only a few minutes he stood up and said, "I don't like this."

He told us that by the fourth month of pregnancy, the uterus is usually distended with water and the heartbeat can be picked up easily. What he saw in me pointed to one thing: Our baby was dead. If he wasn't, the chances of saving him were slim, since my cervix had already begun to dilate. The cramps that had now started coming more steadily were a definite indicator that I was having a miscarriage.

"I suggest we go ahead and do a D & C," he said. "You *could* go home and wait to abort the baby on your own, but that could be painful, and it's definitely not pleasant. Besides, it might take another week, and you'd run the risk of infection. We'd have to do a D & C then anyway."

"Are you sure he's dead?" I asked. I knew I sounded pathetic, but I felt I owed it to the baby to at least ask.

For the first time since the nightmare began, someone seemed to understand.

"Let's do a sonogram," Dr. Myer said, "and then you'll know for sure."

The test proved what we'd all suspected. Instead of the mischievous tadpole, there was a lifeless womb. I started to cry.

"Let's go ahead with it," Jim said.

"It's like losing a child," Dr. Myer told us. "You *will* accept it in time, but this has got to be hard for you. I'm really sorry."

I wanted to hug him.

An hour later my pregnancy was over. When I awoke, Jim was there, telling me that the baby was a boy, and that my bad dream was finally over.

He couldn't know that it was anything but over. It had, in fact, only begun.

THREE

What Happened?

I believe very strongly that our Lord died to take away our sins — not our minds.

We were endowed by the Father with an incredible capacity to think and understand. We can't, of course, comprehend everything He does, but I think when circumstances occur that we can decipher, we ought to use the phenomenal capacity of our brains to understand and then respond appropriately.

Naturally then, the first thing I wanted to know after my miscarriage was, "What happened to cause it?" It's a legitimate question and one that can and should be answered for any victim of a pregnancy loss. Knowing what happened to her body and to her baby can be a real comfort to a mother and her family.

When I started probing for answers, I was amazed to find out that miscarriage is not a horrendous blunder played on us by our body. It is simply one of God's processes, one in which the body responds to crisis by expelling foreign matter, thereby cleansing itself.

What I'm about to explain may be easier to swallow if you understand God's miraculous process of conception and gestation. To acquaint or reacquaint yourself with these stages, glance at

Appendix I before reading on.

SAFETY ESCAPE SYSTEM

In His master plan for reproduction, it makes sense that God would include a safety feature — an alternate plan, if you will — just in case there are sudden dangers to either fetus or mother. With so many delicate yet crucial steps taking place so rapidly, it's easy to see how something could run amuck.

Here's how that "safety escape system" works.

When the fetus or placenta doesn't develop as it should, or a physical problem in the mother persists, the proper biological signals are not sent. The mother's body can't set itself up to protect and nurture the baby for the required nine months. Instead of growing thicker and engorging with blood, the endometrium (the uterus lining that forms and is expelled each month during the menstrual cycle) begins to break apart and slough off. As a result, the placenta detaches, in part or completely, and the fetus doesn't get the nourishment it needs. The uterus has reacted as if there were a foreign body within it. With the magic only God can supply, the uterus contracts and expels the products of pregnancy. If it didn't, infection would occur, and the mother would become very ill.

In my anger and disappointment over losing my baby, I turned on my body and demanded of it, "Why did you malfunction on me?"

But that wasn't fair. It was functioning exactly as it was supposed to *when something goes wrong.*

The physical symptoms the mother experiences before a miscarriage occurs are a direct indication of the activity going on within her body. (For a more detailed explanation, see Appendix II.) Generally speaking, bleeding and cramping are the most common signs of what doctors and nurses call a *threatened abortion.* This means that, although bleeding is taking place, the cervix is still closed, and the fetus remains in the uterus. In 50 percent of the cases, a threatened abortion becomes a miscarriage.

It's never fun to see your body parting with its blood, nor is pain something you invite. But I've found it soothing to remind myself that what took place in my miscarriage was part of God's process for *helping* the baby and me.

Baby Rue needed to exit from a place where he couldn't be cared for. The cramps came as my uterus escorted him out.

I would have become ill if the remains of the pregnancy hadn't been removed, too, and that explains the loss of blood and tissue. A cleansing process took place in order to ready my uterus for another baby.

MEDICAL RESPONSES TO MISCARRIAGE

In the medical field, where it sometimes seems that all things are possible, there are no sure treatments for miscarriage. Preventing miscarriage would be like trying to keep a broken bone from undergoing its natural healing process. Miscarriage happens because something has already gone wrong for the baby, and God is taking him back as efficiently as possible.

Some doctors used to give compounds of progesterone to prevent miscarriage in their patients who threatened to abort. However, that practice is now almost obsolete, for such treatment has been shown to lead to *missed abortion.* The fetus dies but remains in the uterus, with the other products of conception, for four weeks or more. Sometimes this happens even when the mother doesn't take progesterone. The uterus remains stationary, the breasts shrink again, the mother loses weight, and the uterus gets smaller because the amniotic fluid is being absorbed and the fetal tissue softens and separates.

Progesterone treatment just delays the inevitable and increases the chance of infection in the mother. As the trapped tissue decays, brown bleeding continues. All the while, the mother suffers considerable emotional stress.

However, sometimes specific action *can* be taken to prevent a threatened miscarriage. One such instance is in the case of a possible *late abortion,* or a miscarriage that threatens between the twelfth and twentieth weeks of pregnancy. When this occurs, it is often treated differently from a miscarriage that threatens in the first trimester, because a problem with the baby is seldom the cause. Other factors, which can sometimes be treated successfully to save the pregnancy, are usually involved. We'll look at this in more detail later on.

Another instance when an impending miscarriage may be treatable is when the mother has suffered two or more miscarriages previously. This phenomenon is called *habitual abortion,* and more than mere chance is involved here. A doctor who finds a treatable cause for the miscarriages may prescribe treatment early in a subsequent pregnancy to help bring a healthy baby to term.

PREGNANCY LOSSES

Other medical problems that accompany incomplete pregnancies are also categorized under the "abortion" label. For example, when the uterus doesn't empty completely during a miscarriage, it is called an *incomplete abortion.* This condition leaves the cervix somewhat dilated and the uterus open to bacterial invasion. Dying or dead fetal tissue left in the womb is fertile ground for the breeding of bacteria, which could induce a *septic* (infected) *abortion,* discharging the remains of the pregnancy and possibly leading to serious complications.

To treat the incomplete abortion, the uterus must be emptied. This is done by stretching or widening the cervix and either gently scraping the tissue from the uterus with a spoon-shaped instrument called a curette, or suctioning it away from the lining. Most of us know this procedure by its common name, *D & C,* which stands for dilation and curettage. Performed under either a local or general anesthetic, the D & C removes all the products of conception (both the fetus and the placenta) from the uterus.

While performing the D & C, the doctor can check also for congenital abnormalities of the uterus, look for tumors or polyps, and take tissue samples from the fetal remains to pinpoint any diseases that had been developing.

Several weeks after my miscarriage, my husband and I received the inevitable hospital bill, and I was horrified to see that the computer called my D & C a "therapeutic abortion." Even though we were certain that William Bradley was already dead, a sickening sense of guilt set in.

But no woman who has completed a miscarriage by having a D & C need feel that she has murdered her baby. A physician will not perform the procedure unless he or she is certain that the mother is no longer pregnant. He'll do it only to be sure that the process God started is cleanly finished. It is *not* an elected abortion.

After a miscarriage, physical recovery time is usually short. Cramps for a day or two are common and are the result of the contractions of the uterine muscles. A discharge of lochia (blood from the uterus) will also continue for a while. It will be bright red at first, decreasing to brown staining within a short time.

After a second trimester miscarriage, the breasts may be engorged with milk, which usually causes a would-be mother a great deal of emotional pain as well as physical discomfort. She should resist the temptation to express the milk to alleviate the pressure; that will only increase its production. Taking aspirins or applying hot, wet compresses or ice packs usually does the trick.

Two other kinds of early pregnancy loss deserve mention here as well.

One involves a *hydatidiform mole* and occurs in one out of 2,000 pregnancies in the United States. Early in the pregnancy, the placenta, which forms to draw nutrients and oxygen from the mother's blood, develops instead into blisters filled with watery fluid. The placenta becomes a "tumor" shaped like a large cluster of grapes, and the fetus doesn't develop at all.[1] The condition is described as "a temporary missed abortion of a blighted ovum," or *blighted ovum*. Eighty percent of these moles are expelled about the twentieth week of pregnancy.[2]

In a molar pregnancy, the uterus may enlarge more rapidly than usual, exceeding the expected size for the age of the baby, and no fetal heartbeat will be found. While this usually causes the mother no pain, the presence of a mole can possibly lead to cancer, so the mother is watched carefully afterward. As we shall see later, the emotional ramifications of a blighted ovum can be the most painful part of this pregnancy loss.

Another kind of early pregnancy loss is the *ectopic pregnancy*. While this is not a miscarriage, many mothers experience the same emotional reactions as those who do miscarry. An ectopic pregnancy (also called a *tubal pregnancy*) occurs when the fertilized egg implants in a place other than the uterus. Usually it nests in a Fallopian tube, but occasionally it can attach to a wall in the ovaries, the cervix or the abdomen. In any case, this is a life-threatening situation that nearly always requires surgery.

Even before the pregnancy is confirmed, the pain of the embryo pushing on the tiny Fallopian tube can be great. An ectopic pregnancy is detected most often within four weeks after conception. If the growing embryo breaks through the tubal wall or the primitive placenta invades and erodes the blood vessels of the tube, a "tubal rupture" occurs and internal hemorrhaging follows.

The mother may or may not miss a period before she notices scanty, dark brown bleeding. She may become faint and weak and will invariably feel much pain. An examination by a doctor may reveal low blood pressure, a tender pelvic mass, high pulse and a low body temperature.[3] An ectopic pregnancy is difficult to diagnose, but once a doctor is certain of it, the move to the operating table will be swift, because the hemorrhage that follows the rupture of a Fallopian tube can be fatal.[4]

If the diagnosis of an ectopic pregnancy is made before the tube ruptures, it is possible to remove the embryo surgically without removing the tube. Usually, however, a *salpingectomy* (removal of the tube) is required. If one Fallopian tube has ruptured and the other tube is missing or damaged, the surgeon may do reconstructive surgery on the ruptured tube, but that increases the chance of another ectopic pregnancy.[5]

By conveying information on the various medical conditions that often spur miscarriage, I'm certainly not suggesting that just knowing what happened in any of these circumstances makes everything all right in a devastated mother's mind. I know from experience that when you're in the midst of a loss, you don't want to hear a rendition of how wonderful the Lord is to have provided a system for taking care of babies who die before they're born! But later, sometimes much later, the news can be comforting.

Having a miscarriage is something most of us never forget. But when we remember, the image of a baby cradled in the arms of a loving God is a sweeter vision than that of one struggling for life in an unfriendly womb.

PART TWO

Why Did It Happen?

*For now we see in a mirror
dimly, but then face to face;
now I know in part, but then I
shall know fully just as I also
have been fully known.*
                1 Corinthians 13:12

FOUR

What *Doesn't* Cause a Miscarriage?

It's one thing to understand the process of miscarriage, but quite another to comprehend why it happened. Why didn't the baby develop properly? Why didn't the placenta provide the necessary goodies to keep him alive? Why did something go wrong that triggered a spontaneous abortion? Doggone it, *Why?*

After my miscarriage, I was plagued with whys, yet I felt guilty about that, too. I was a Christian, after all, so shouldn't I just accept the miscarriage as God's will and get on with life?

Fortunately, the minister of our church gave me some food for thought in that area.

"Why do you think God gave you that good mind of yours?" he barked at me. "You're a teacher. You're a writer. You're obviously a very intelligent woman. Where do you think you got all those gifts?"

I meekly murmured, "From God."

"All right, then! You're using your smarts for God's glory. Do you think He expects you to turn them off when a crisis hits? For heaven's sake, no!"

As I thought about his words, I had to agree. We are a people who believe in reason and logic, and cause and effect — as well as in divine intervention and the power of the Holy Spirit.

God has commanded us to think and reason, and He has given us the mental capacity to do it. If we were meant merely to watch and shrug our shoulders as diseases destroyed flesh and as psychological problems disintegrated minds — and as miscarriages swept away much-wanted babies — we would be no more intelligent than your basic sparrow.

Questioning doesn't indicate we're challenging God's authority. Our loving Father has given us questioning minds to help us find meaning. By asking why, we learn and grow. "Curiosity," wrote William Kotzwinkle in *Swimmer in the Secret Sea*, "moves the world forward, closer to the creator."[1]

Finding out why — or more important, why not — also eliminates much of the anxiety, confusion and unnecessary guilt feelings that surface in the aftermath of a miscarriage.

When I went in for a checkup four weeks after my loss, Dr. Breeden said to me, "I want to be sure you don't think it was anything you did or didn't do that caused the baby to die. Sometimes I have a hard time convincing people — husbands, too — that a woman doesn't cause her own miscarriage."

Over and over, doctors who have written articles or kindly responded to my interview questions have said: It's no one's fault. As hard as it is for us to believe in this world of pointing fingers, sometimes things happen and no one is to blame.

But it is surprising how many ideas we've accepted about miscarriage that are simply not true.

To set your mind at ease, these things do *not* cause early pregnancy loss:

EXCESSIVE PHYSICAL ACTIVITY

"A healthy pregnancy hangs on regardless of whether you hang curtains or stay in bed," says Richard Schwarz, chairman of the Department of Obstetrics and Gynecology at State University of New York.[2]

God provides maximum protection for a baby in the womb. A cushion of amniotic fluid, which is itself shielded from physical assault by the amniotic sac, surrounds him, as does the muscular wall of the uterus and the mother's abdominal organs and skin. Most women, unless they have other physical defects, can work, travel and exercise in moderation during pregnancy with no risk to their babies or themselves.

Wanda was convinced, even twenty years after the fact, that she caused her first miscarriage by scraping paint off their garage. "It was all that stretching and reaching and climbing up and down the ladder that did it," she told me, and nothing I said would change her mind. I wish I could have convinced her, because twenty years of guilt could have been eased away if only she'd have believed me!

PHYSICAL INJURY OR TRAUMA

Soap operas and melodramatic movies are probably largely responsible for the myth that a fall or physical accident is a direct cause of a miscarriage.

Physical trauma is considered to be a very unlikely reason for miscarriage because of what is now known about the way the baby is protected in the uterus and because of countless physical traumas which have *not* caused spontaneous abortion. In only one case in a thousand is physical injury the culprit, and then the injury must be severe.

SEXUAL ACTIVITY

Sometimes the bleeding associated with a miscarriage starts soon after a couple has had sexual intercourse, and that can cause real emotional distress, especially for husbands, who then view themselves as lustful killers who couldn't control their passions.

The report by the American College of Obstetricians and Gynecologists published in June 1985 states, "There is no evidence that physical activity or sex causes miscarriage."[3] As fertility specialist Sherwin Kaufman put it, "If miscarriage was caused by intercourse, the birth rate would drop to zero."[4]

PSYCHOLOGICAL REASONS

After my miscarriage, I wondered for a long time if my anguished worrying through sleepless nights caused Baby Rue's death. Now I know that it is extremely unlikely.

Over the years psychologists have suggested that fear of pregnancy, marital conflicts, neuroses, and hostility toward one's *mother* (!) cause miscarriages. But no real evidence exists that proves emotional upset or psychological problems of any kind cause fetal loss. Until recently, the medical community has tended to blame women's problems that they haven't understood on their supposed psychological ills.

In cases where sudden emotional disturbances were thought to be the cause of a miscarriage, examination of the baby and placenta revealed defects that occurred *before* the mother suffered her emotional distress. Regardless of what happens on "As the World Turns," psychic factors are not to blame.

HEREDITARY FACTORS

One common misconception says that miscarriages run in families. This is not true. I felt like the black sheep of my family when I lost a baby after my mother and sister carried every child to term like hardy peasant women. But miscarriage could have happened to them, too. Family history has nothing to do with it.

PRIOR USE OF CONTRACEPTIVES

Taking oral contraceptives (like the pill) before conceiving, or wearing an IUD that is removed prior to conception, doesn't cause a miscarriage in a subsequent pregnancy. Although one study showed a possible connection between spermicidal contraceptives (jellies, creams and foams) and miscarriage, recent studies reveal no such association. Even one previously induced abortion hasn't been shown to cause a miscarriage in the next pregnancy.

PERSONAL CARE

A woman suffering from extreme malnutrition (rare in the United States) *might* miscarry for nutritional reasons. However, thoughts like *I didn't eat right* or *I didn't get enough sleep* should be banished. Those actions aren't at fault.

A doctor sometimes advises a patient who is threatening to abort to stay in bed. Authorities on the subject aren't sure this does much to prevent a miscarriage, so a woman who subsequently loses her baby shouldn't blame herself if she climbed out of bed to change the channel on the TV. The miscarriage would have happened anyway.

PUNISHMENT BY GOD

There probably isn't one Christian family affected by miscarriage who, in searching for reasons, hasn't heard or considered this thought: *This is God's punishment.*

When Gerry became pregnant the third time, she did her

share of moaning over the spacing — or lack of it! — between her two toddlers and the new baby. When she miscarried at four and a half months, she was certain God had punished her for feeling that way.

Tricia, a close high school friend of mine, wasn't "altogether ecstatic" about being pregnant. Her daughter Katie was five, and Tricia was experiencing some freedom at last. When her pregnancy ended at twelve weeks, she wondered if her feelings prompted God to take the baby away.

I shared many of those feelings. What if I had wanted William Bradley right from the start? What if I'd had no doubts, no mixed feelings? What if I'd passively accepted my surprise pregnancy as God's will and turned a shining face to the world? And what about the way I sometimes treated Marijean? Did God know from the way I lost my temper with her and smacked her fingers for overturning the begonias that I wasn't fit to have more children?

I have learned since then that that kind of thinking is more Old Testament than New Testament. Let me explain.

God, as He is described in Old Testament books such as Deuteronomy and 1 and 2 Chronicles, rewarded obedience to the law and punished disobedience. Sinners among the Jews who were forgiven worked to receive grace. They also faced judgment and accepted punishment.

How different this is from the picture of God which we see in the New Testament in the "age of grace." He forgives endlessly, seventy times seven, if only we believe in and trust in Him. God keeps no score sheet on us. The image of God meting out one miscarriage for every mistake a mother makes is pretty far afield from the God the Bible describes.

No, says the psalmist in Psalm 50:14, don't bother offering burnt offerings — or unborn babies — to Yahweh. "What I want from you is your true thanks; I want your promises fulfilled" (TLB). God won't take anything else from you.

If none of these things we've looked at — including God's wrath — causes miscarriage, then what does?

No conclusive answers exist. Sometimes the reason for a fetal loss is never known. But knowing some facts about pregnancy and miscarriage can comfort a woman who loses a baby.

FIVE

Are There
Any Answers?

"I need to take this one back and keep him in My tender care. He just wouldn't make it there with you."

That's what God seems to say when a miscarriage occurs. "Why?" we ask. We don't always know why, and that can be frustrating. We assume that miracle drugs will heal us and our doctors will have all the answers, and we forget that doctors only cooperate with nature. It's *God* who remains in charge, with reasons of His own that we can never hope to comprehend.[1]

What we do know about the medical reasons for miscarriage is certainly worth understanding. Medical problems fall into two categories: (1) *fetal factors*, such as defects in the baby, the placenta, or the membranes that surround the baby and hold the water he floats in; and (2) *maternal factors*, caused by physical defects in the mother that interfere with her ability to carry her baby to term.

If a miscarriage occurs in the early months of a pregnancy, it is almost always preceded by the death of the fetus, which indicates that the problem is probably with the baby or his environment. If a fetus survives its first few months of the pregnancy and then a miscarriage occurs, the loss is probably directly related to problems in the mother's system.[2] (That doesn't mean, however, that the mother *did* anything wrong.)

FETAL FACTORS

Let's look at some of the problems that can plague a pregnancy. In 50 to 60 percent of cases where fetuses miscarry before the twelfth week, *chromosomal abnormalities* exist in the fetus.

Every normal cell consists of 46 paired chromosomes. These sticky strands contain *genes*, the genetic information that determines what we are, including eye and hair color, length of our big toe, and everything else about us. When the sperm fertilizes the egg, each donates 23 strands. But sometimes the correct number of strands are "tampered with" during the fertilization process. Some studies show this is more likely if the sperm fertilizes an "aging" egg, one that is already several days past ovulation.

Once the egg is fertilized, it immediately divides to make that miracle, a tiny person. Sometimes something goes wrong when these early divisions take place. (One theory supposes that sections of chromosomal strands stick together instead of separating.[3]) Whatever error occurs multiplies in the millions of cells that grow from it. Whole lines of cells mutate, and the normal growth pattern of the infant becomes disorganized. Eventually, if the mother's rejection system is alert, the pregnancy aborts.[4]

Usually the abnormal characteristic was carried in either the egg or sperm and was present before the two joined. We all inherit a certain number of problem genes from our parents. They can be recessive, which means they're never expressed, or of minor importance to our general health, coming out in something like nearsightedness. Or they can be fatal to a fetus. If one of those problem genes is crucial to the survival of the baby, the abnormality will kill the baby or at least cause a major disruption in its normal growth process. In either case, the pregnancy usually aborts.

If a baby with an abnormal number of chromosomes is born alive at the end of a pregnancy, he or she will have serious birth defects, or will be mentally retarded, or both. For example, Down's syndrome occurs when one too many chromosomes exists.

Chromosomal problems that cause a woman to miscarry are genetic accidents 95 percent of the time, especially when the same woman has had one or more live births.[5] That's because the occurrence of the chromosomal defects, or *random mutation*, is largely happenstance. Suzanne, who's had three children since her first miscarriage, and Jean, who's had two, are not likely to experience the same problem again. The odds are less than one in a million that random mutation would happen twice for the same couple.[6]

Of course, there are factors that increase the chances of these mistakes occurring. Age is one. As a couple grows older, there's a greater likelihood of a chromosomal error, simply because a woman's eggs are older. Environmental factors, called *teratogens*, are another consideration. We'll look at more information on both of these factors later.

Cells that make up an infant must not only have the right number of chromosomes, but the chromosomes also must be arranged in proper order. Of the miscarriages that result from chromosomal abnormalities, 5 percent are due to abnormalities in the structure, rather than in the number, of the chromosomes.[7] The order of information in the genetic code is vital. If that order is off in either the egg or sperm, this is called a *balanced translocation*, and, unfortunately, it isn't just "bad luck." It's part of the permanent genetic structure of one or both parents.[8]

If a woman has two or more miscarriages interspersed with live births, a translocation is usually suspected, and couples are advised to participate in genetic counseling. This doesn't mean that they should not continue trying to have children. But it will give them an idea of the possible risks they face and the odds that the woman will miscarry again.

Genetic counseling includes the study of a couple's chromosomes, which costs about $300. Blood is drawn from each partner. The cells are then examined and a picture is taken of the chromosomes. The picture, called an *idiogram* or *karyotype*, is analyzed for errors in the normal number, size and arrangement of the chromosomal material, and it reveals whether either parent carries a translocation.

Chromosomes are not always the culprits of early-pregnancy miscarriages. It may be that nothing is wrong with the baby, but that problems exist in the environment he lives in.

MATERNAL FACTORS

In order for the fetus to nest properly in the uterus, many things must take place in perfect coordination, including hormone secretions, glandular processes, and the sending of certain biological signals that keep the baby alive. If any one element fails, the baby's survival is endangered and a spontaneous abortion threatens. The process is so intricate, it's amazing that successful implantation occurs as often as it does![9]

All may be well with the baby and his environment but still a miscarriage may occur. It could be that the mother has problems that make it impossible for her to carry her baby to term. Fortunately, this is very unusual. Only in cases of repeated and consecutive miscarriages do doctors look at this as a possibility. If this is your situation or that of someone you know, read Appendix III, which highlights some of the major problems.

Researchers are checking out the following ten factors as possible causes for miscarriage (none of these has been proven to cause fetal loss, but all are being considered in current studies):

(1) *The mother's age.* The older the mother, the more likely her chances of miscarrying. The risk of having a miscarriage in the first trimester nearly doubles after the age of thirty, and doubles again after thirty-five. Of every 1,000 pregnancies in women aged thirty to thirty-four, 75 end in miscarriage. After the age of thirty-five the rate rises to 150 per 1,000.

In an older mother, the eggs are often "overripe." An increased chance of hormonal imbalance and an irregular menstrual cycle delay the timing of ovulation and fertilization.

(2) *The mother's weight.* Several studies show that women with serious weight problems, weighing 200 pounds or more, have twice as many miscarriages as other women.[10]

(3) *Treatment for infertility.* The medical field has discovered many successful ways to help childless couples become pregnant, but some of these methods may increase the chances of miscarriage. Medications such as Clomid that induce ovulation are suspect (miscarriage rates double)[11] and after tubal surgery, miscarriage rates rise 20 percent.

(4) *Environmental factors.* Direct contact with any of the following teratogens can bring about developmental defects in a fetus in its very early stages and perhaps cause a miscarriage: certain hormones, including those found in oral contraceptives; plastics; petroleum products; radiation (X rays); anesthetics; alcohol; caffeine; tobacco; nitrous oxide (exposure doubles the miscarriage rate); lead; carbon disulfide (a cleaning solvent); chloroprene (used in rubber production); herbicide 2-4-5-T (used by lumbering firms in the Northwest); pesticides; toxic household chemicals; and certain drugs, including quinine. Women who live in neighborhoods near foundries and who are exposed to smelter emissions or who are married to men who work with these products also run a higher than average incidence of miscarriage.

(5) *The IUD.* Of women who become pregnant while using an IUD and who leave it in place during the pregnancy, 52 to 57 percent lose their babies in miscarriage. If the IUD is expelled or removed *shortly* after conception, the incidence of miscarriage is reduced to between 20 and 25 percent. After thirteen weeks of an apparently normal pregnancy, the danger of miscarriage drops to 6 percent if the IUD has been removed, and rises to 26 percent if it hasn't.[12]

    Researchers don't yet know whether the IUD causes an abnormality in the developing baby or whether it makes proper implantation in the uterus more difficult. The facts aren't in yet.[13]

(6) *Amniocentesis.* This is a test done in some high-risk pregnancies to test the amniotic fluid that surrounds the fetus for possible abnormalities in the baby or his environment. Because a syringe is used to extract fluid from the sac, there is a 1-in-200 chance that the membrane will prematurely rupture and cause a miscarriage.[14] However, risk diminishes when ultrasound is used to guide the insertion of the syringe.

(7) *Conization.* This surgical procedure diagnoses cervical cancer and is useful for treating certain conditions of the cervix. Of women who become pregnant after conization, 25 percent miscarry.[15]

(8) *Alcohol.* The risk of miscarriage increases significantly with the ingestion of alcohol during pregnancy. Women who drink even as little as one ounce of absolute alcohol twice a week push their miscarriage rate from 10 percent to between 15 and 35 percent.[16] The adverse effects seem more likely with wine and spirits than with beer. However, consumption equal to two ounces per week of any absolute alcohol can produce acute fetal poisoning. It's likely that the reproductive process is highly sensitive to alcohol and that miscarriage is the most frequent evidence of that.[17]

(9) *Smoking.* Controversy continues over whether smoking increases the rate of miscarriage. However, many researchers report that the miscarriage rate is almost twice as high among smokers as nonsmokers, and the incidence increases with the number of cigarettes smoked.[18]

(10) *Previous induced abortions.* Women who have had two or more induced abortions double — sometimes triple — their chances of losing a baby in the first trimester.

    Induced abortions that are done by the D & C method create more risk of later miscarriage than those done by vacuum aspiration (where the fetus is suctioned through a hose that works much like a vacuum cleaner).[19] It may be that repeated curettage creates abnormalities in the uterus lining that can prevent implantation. This does not mean that a woman who has had multiple abortions can't carry a baby to term. It simply means that her chances for miscarrying are higher.

No part of this discussion is intended to produce guilt! No one knows for sure what brings about a miscarriage. There is no way of knowing whether fetal loss would have occurred in the absence of *all* of them. My own case speaks well to that.

I was using an IUD when I became pregnant with William Bradley. Shortly after my miscarriage, a well-meaning friend said to me, "You know, an IUD doesn't prevent pregnancy by keeping sperm from fertilizing the egg. It just makes your uterus an undesirable place for the fertilized egg to implant. You could have been conceiving and having little spontaneous abortions every month without ever knowing it! It really isn't surprising that you didn't go to term."

I was stunned. It was months before I could think of anything else except the possibility that I had killed my own baby. Had he been in there fighting for his life? Had he been trying to hold on to the mother who was supposed to nurture him and protect him but who had been murdering his brothers and sisters for two and a half years and really wanted him out of the way, too?

COMFORT OF FAITH

I might have flipped out entirely if another friend hadn't jolted me back to reality. "So how do you explain what happened to Barb?" she said to me one day as I cried over the phone.

"Barb?"

"That girl we taught with at Carson High. She had a baby with an IUD in place the whole time. She had images of Missy being born with the thing in her hand, laughing her head off!"

Why did one "IUD baby" die and another live? I couldn't help but wonder, *Was it something I did?*

Now I'm sure the answer is no. No doctor has ever said to me, "You lost the baby because of the IUD." So many factors worked together that it's impossible to tell what caused the baby's death.

Jim and I accepted the fact that we were using an IUD as a contraceptive because that seemed the best thing for us to do at the time. In spite of our initial doubts about my second pregnancy, we loved our baby even before we knew about him, because we love each other.

I mention these factors which may contribute to miscarriage merely as guidelines for future pregnancies. Even then, the factors could cause a fetal loss no matter how careful Mom and Dad are.

It's then that we must lean back on that always-ready, always-comforting cushion called faith.

Even the most scientific person can't hope to find all the answers to life's questions. In his search for truth, he won't always get them. His job is to seek those answers with all his might. But he is blessed if he can say what Jesus said to His Father at Gethsemane, "Let it be as You, not I, would have it" (Mark 14:36).[20]

In his book *Why Us? When Bad Things Happen To God's People*, Warren Wiersbe says that Christians live by promises, not by explanations. Even if God answered all our questions, the answers aren't guaranteed to make life easier or loss more bearable. People need God, he says, far more than they need explanations.[21]

When all reasons for the loss of an unborn baby have been exhausted, we can still say, "I don't understand, Lord. In time I hope I can be satisfied with, 'You must have had Your reasons.'"

PART THREE

How Can We Deal With It?

*"Screams of anguish
    come from Ramah,
Weeping unrestrained;
Rachel weeping for her
    children,
Uncomforted —
For they are dead."*
        Matthew 2:18 (TLB)

SIX

Should I Feel
as Bad as I Do?

In that bleak time after our baby died, I felt so many different, painful, frightening things all at once.

Physically, I felt exhausted. Every function was an effort punctuated by sighs of grief that rose up from the depths of me. My chest ached from holding back a flood of tears; I was afraid I wouldn't be able to stop if I really let them go. My arms felt heavy and cumbersome. I slept poorly, and my appetite dwindled to nothing.

Emotionally, I fluctuated between feelings of numbness and feelings that seemed alive with hurt. I listened to entire conversations and walked away not having a clue to what had been said or even to what I had said. I stared at my students' papers that needed to be graded and couldn't comprehend a word. I laughed on cue, but the sound was hard and flat. I put clothes in the washer and made beef stew and tied Marijean's shoes, all with the enthusiasm of a robot. And when I saw how weary and crippled with sadness I was, I got scared.

After all, it was "only a miscarriage." I hadn't even come close to death. Jim was still there. Marijean was beside me. Everyone was acting as if life should be continuing as usual. *I simply must be losing my grip,* I thought. I felt sure I needed massive psychiatric help.

Because I couldn't cheer myself up, I was forced to allow myself the right to grieve. My usual ways of coping with tough situations, like having my hair cut or rearranging the furniture, didn't work this time. I couldn't do anything but mourn.

And that was exactly what I needed to do.

I know now that I had a right to grieve. Anyone who has been touched by the loss of a pregnancy does. "You feel rotten!" my friend Suzanne told me. "You have a right to feel rotten. So if you want to feel rotten for two months, do it!"

Those were probably the kindest words anyone said to me. In contrast, one week — *one week* — after William died, a co-worker approached me and asked when I was going to be the old Nancy Rue they all knew and loved. That same afternoon I stopped at a friend's house, and she said, "You have to get ahold of this thing. I watched you walking up my front walk just now, and I could have scraped you up with a spatula, you were so low."

Although at the time I wanted to scream at both of them, I realize now that they only reflected our society's all-too-common tendency to deny a mourning family its right to grieve over anything, including a lost baby.

Our culture is "death-denying" and "death-defying," writes one pastor.[1] Very few people understand grief of any kind, and when it's expressed in its most agonizing form, many are frightened. It's much more comfortable to deny death and reject grief.

When well-meaning relatives say, "At least you have other children," or "You can always have another one," their comments imply that your loss is insignificant. When society refuses to admit that your baby died and that you suffered a real loss, your behavior can look rather bizarre. But mourning can't take its normal course when we think our grief is abnormal. And the truth is, it isn't.

The greatest gift I can give to a victim of miscarriage is to convince her that her loss is real, and that she can and should grieve until she can accept it and go on. If she views her loss as an experience she must simply live through, then she should allow herself to do that. If she feels her world has suddenly been emptied out, ransacked and stomped on, she should let herself feel that, too.

TWO RULES FOR GRIEVING

It's common for friends to try to assuage grief with comments like, "At least you're not as bad off as that lady down the street who lost all five of her children in a fire." But Rule #1 for grieving is: *Don't compare your loss to someone else's.* I ask God's forgiveness for sins less awful than those other people commit, and I ask His grace in situations less desperate than those others are in. Why, then, shouldn't I hurt just as deeply and pray just as hard for God's help in my loss as one who loses a husband, a five-year-old, or a full-term stillborn baby?

Rule #2: *Give yourself permission to grieve.* Grief is a human reaction to any loss. It's not an emotion reserved for the death of someone you knew twenty years or someone you touched and held in your arms. It occurs when you're deprived of someone or something in which you have invested a part of yourself. What did you and your husband put more of yourselves into than the dream of your child? A parent who loses a child in pregnancy, no matter how early, is bereaved.[2]

Whether you experience an ectopic pregnancy, an early trimester miscarriage or the ending of a pregnancy at twenty-eight weeks, that was a baby you were carrying. The moment the sperm fertilized the egg, new life began. "It is a man and not a thing," wrote Karl Barth, "not a mere part of the mother's body."[3]

A dream is also gone. From the day you found out you were pregnant, no matter how shocked you were, you imagined how this little baby would change your life. If the pregnancy was carefully planned or long-awaited, a dream already had begun to come true.

Even couples who are never able to conceive feel intense disappointment and grief at times, mourning for all the children that will never be born to them.[4] A dream is hard to relinquish.

You lose part of yourself as well. That first trimester of pregnancy is a narcissistic time. As comedian Bill Cosby says, though that baby doesn't even have a face yet, he is part of you. He gives you morning sickness, he forces you to take three naps a day, and he wakes you up in the middle of the night to go to the bathroom. You and another person are one, and you feel total responsibility for nourishing and protecting him.

As a pregnant woman, you also enjoy a special, treasured spotlight. When you lose your pregnancy, that "specialness" vanishes too. Your raised self-esteem and your confidence in your ability to nurture also disappear. Elizabeth Fuller, author, and victim of two miscarriages after years of infertility, writes, "When nature turns on you, *that* is the ultimate rejection slip."[5]

Grief is greatest, of course, because you loved your baby. You were his mother, and he was someone you fell in love with the way no one else ever could. There is no human relationship where the body identification of one person is so close to another as in the process of pregnancy.[6] God intended for it to be fierce and protective, and for you and your unborn child to have an intense intimacy.

"Grief," writes Rev. Edgar Jackson, "is the other side of the coin of love."[7] When you love someone as much as you already love your baby, powerful emotions culminate when he dies. The meaning of life itself is fractured for a time as you experience deep despair, and such despair is different from any other.

POINTS TO REMEMBER

Even after you acknowledge that you lost someone important, several factors can make your loss unique and more difficult to face than the death of someone who has walked and talked and breathed. Understanding the following points can help you "go a little easier" on yourself:

(1) *It's hard to say the word "death" when you haven't even given birth.* Accept the difficulty, and let it be OK.

(2) *Remember that pregnancy alone is an important life crisis, full of major emotional and physical changes right from the start.* Usually these changes are resolved by the birth of the baby. When there is no birth, the pregnancy crisis runs headlong into the crisis of your baby's death. Your world view, which changed when you became pregnant, changes again when the baby dies, and it will never be quite the same again. You may become unstable, vulnerable, anxious. Suddenly, you don't seem able to trust anybody, not even God. Remember: Such feelings are normal.

(3) *You are cheated out of the triumphant moment of birth.* "Even the humblest woman is exalted by carrying life," Marjorie Holmes writes.[8] You wait for that magnificent moment when you can hold your baby next to you and say, "I am your mom." There is no climax when you miscarry. You barely make it a third of the way to your goal. What you have when it's over is plain old emptiness.

(4) *A pregnancy loss may be your first encounter with death, so your grieving skills my be undeveloped.* We must *learn* how to grieve and, unfortunately, it comes only with practice. Learning is difficult.

(5) *A miscarriage is often sudden and unpredictable, and that kind of loss is always more difficult to deal with than one you've prepared yourself for.* When you become pregnant,

you assume you will deliver a healthy baby in a few months. When your baby dies, you are naturally surprised, and probably frightened and overwhelmed at how in just a few hours, everything has changed.

Barbara Berg, a writer and college professor who suffered the loss of two babies, says it well. "Pregnant and full and hopeful one day, empty and fragmented the next. And with no real understanding or acceptance of what had happened in between," she writes. "Everything was cut short, unfulfilled, unfinished, and every part of me screamed for completion."[9]

(6) *No funeral or memorial service follows the miscarriage to help you work through your grief.* Such rituals give the bereaved a chance to say good-bye. Without them, your loss seems unreal.

(7) *As if all this weren't enough, your grief is also harder to cope with because of your weakened physical condition.* You may be weak from loss of blood. Anemia is common after a miscarriage. Perhaps you feel numb from the medication given to you during and after your D & C. Your body changed while you were pregnant, and now it's working hard to get back to your normal state. Your hormones crash in on you, and you're left with a case of the baby blues, with no baby to compensate.

(8) *If you have other children, you may experience guilt because you can't say, "I'm just grateful for what I have."* There is nothing wrong with that. Having living children doesn't diminish grief over the child who has died, nor does your sadness mean you love your living children any less.

(9) *If your loss was an ectopic pregnancy, you may have several worries.* You have a scar, perhaps a lost tube, and maybe even the loss of your ability ever to conceive again — as well as the loss of your baby. And you have all this to cope with *while recovering from major surgery.* Take the time you need to mourn each of the things that is important to you.

(10) *If you had a blighted ovum, you may struggle with the questions, Was I ever really pregnant? Do I have a right to be sad?* Remember: If you feel sad over the baby that almost was, that's your right. Go ahead and cry if you want to.

CHRISTIANS AND GRIEF

Ironically, Christians sometimes suffer more from miscarriage than non-Christians. When our son died, my relationship with the Lord was just beginning. Like many believers, I immaturely thought that feelings like anger and depression were always sinful. *If I believe that God brings everything together for good, shouldn't I just accept William's death and go happily on with my life, secure in my faith?*

I couldn't ignore death, and neither can mature Christians. Now I know that God doesn't intend for us to. Sadness and depression don't signify that a person has little faith. Nowhere in the Bible does it say that Christians are immune to tears and sorrow when someone dies.[10] In fact, the Scriptures record accounts of faithful people who experienced great grief in the face of sorrow, and they expressed it. Even Job, whom we often think of as a stoic, cried out to God in his pain.

Actually, the feelings that come naturally when you miscarry are feelings that God created. Jesus felt agony, fear, pain and sorrow. If we want to be like Him, we must experience and express those feelings, too.

If you sort through your feelings and "put on" only those you approve of, you do yourself an injustice. It is true that if we fully understood God's love and plan for our lives, we'd always be hopeful and peaceful. But we are not yet the kind of people we want to be. We can't understand completely. God doesn't expect us to. He wants us to be honest about how we *do* feel.

But as the apostle Paul says, we do not sorrow as the unsaved do. Our tears, and even our angry words, are tinged with hope, and our motivation to reconcile our grief comes from the Lord. Our heavenly Father gives you the right to grieve. Now let's find out how to do it.

SEVEN

How Do We Grieve?

Although everyone expresses grief in his (or her) own way and recovers at his own pace, the basic experiences a person goes through while mourning are similar. God set the grieving process up so that we will emerge from the seemingly endless dark tunnel of sadness into a clearing where new things have been learned and an entirely new person seems to exist.

Let me tell you what happens when you try to skip the long process of grieving and, therefore, healing.

After our baby died, I grieved but was always keenly aware of "how well I was doing." I asked Jim repeatedly, "Do you think I'm handling this OK?" I beamed when people said they admired my courage. I was devastated when others saw my blacker moments and told me I needed to pull myself together.

I did a lot of things right. I searched for answers to take away my guilt. I talked about my feelings to sympathetic listeners, and I genuinely looked for comfort from God.

But I was terrified at the emptiness and sadness I felt, and I thought that if I could somehow channel my yearnings for my lost baby in another direction, I'd "get over it."

While I was waist-deep in my search for answers, I was also

looking for a new job. When I learned that a new high school was opening up five miles from our house, I applied immediately for a teaching position.

Never mind if that meant leaping out of the stew pot and into the open gas flame! Never mind that accepting a new position would stall my dream of writing at home full time. Never mind that I'd barely had time to recover from my loss and shouldn't be making critical decisions. Instead I saw a new job as a new challenge, a boost to my flagging self-esteem. *It will take my mind off my hurt,* I reasoned.

I was hired, not only as a teacher, but as chairman of the Language and Fine Arts Department. I was given carte blanche and told to write a curriculum, order my books and set up the department. I did, and I spent the entire summer preparing the perfect program.

But after school started I became restless again. It wasn't a good idea, I decided, to bury myself in teaching. So I finished writing my first book and found a publisher. I became involved in the church as never before. I took up long-distance running and ran a half-marathon.

I couldn't do enough to fill up my life. I never stopped loving Jim and Marijean, but slowly they took a place of less importance in my life. It hurt to give myself to them.

In the fall of my second year at Dayton High, I crashed. All the unresolved grief that had festered for almost two years exploded, and I was in deep trouble.

FACING THE TRUTH

It was like reliving William's death, but this time there was no tangible object to grieve over. I couldn't sleep. The thought of eating made me nauseous. My concentration evaporated, and my body pumped with anxiety. All I could do was pace and wring my hands.

I had a complete physical examination that revealed nothing. Anxiously I searched my marriage and my career for signs of stress. They were there, of course, but they weren't the root of the problem.

One morning after tossing in agony all night, I collapsed in Jim's arms. Gently he pulled me away from him and looked at me.

"You want our baby back, don't you?" he said.

My world fell apart, and at last I cried until I couldn't cry any more. He was right. I was still as anguished as I was the day the baby died. I'd never resolved my grief.

That wasn't the end. Next came painful career decisions, the rebuilding of my badly damaged marriage and the reconstruction of my relationship with my daughter. It felt almost overwhelming, and the realization that I couldn't possibly do it alone made it even worse.

For the first time in my life I turned to God and said, "I'm Yours. I can't do it without You. I'm broken. I've messed it up. Please . . . help me."

It took a long time. First I had to go back and live through the sadness I had tried to bury almost two years before. It could have been over. I could have been healed from the hurt and have recovered in a productive, healthy way. But I had to go back and practically start over.

I did heal finally, with God's help. He gave me the courage to give up my teaching position and take the risk of writing full time and facing the isolation of that job that would give me time to think. He forced me to face Jim and express honest feelings, rather than the ones I thought would make me look good in his eyes. Probably most important of all, He led me to give more time and energy to mothering again, even though tenderly touching Marijean and singing to her and meeting her childlike needs reminded me, painfully at first, of what I missed with my infant son.

Healing from a miscarriage doesn't have to be so hard. Grieving for your lost baby can be a growing experience, something that helps get you through the pain — not around it — and on to a better, stronger, wiser you.

I'd like to look with you now at the normal stages of grief. You will be able to see that what you're going through is normal, and that there is hope at the end of it.

As you read, though, try not to intellectualize your grief. Just *feel* it. Avoid the temptation to say, "Oh, so this is just the anger phase. I'll get over it." If you're angry, feel angry! Tell God how angry you are! There can be no clear thinking without allowing for the expression of your emotions.[1]

Don't worry if you don't follow the "steps" in order. They come in waves that seem to have no logic. Don't be concerned, either, if you backslide and find yourself crying again. Things like baby shower invitations, Pampers commercials, the anniversary of your miscarriage or your due date can bring back the depression in full force. The feelings do come back, but never as intensely as at first, and never staying very long. There is no agenda or timetable. Your active grieving could last from several weeks to many months.

Here are the stages of grief:

SHOCK

Whether you call it denial, disbelief or just the numb phase, this is the point where you shake your head and say, "No! This isn't happening to us and our baby."

Jean sensitively described her denial when she miscarried at three months.

"I was so scared, but at the same time refused to give up hope. Even after we got to the hospital and the doctor confirmed that I was having a miscarriage, I thought maybe he could somehow stop what was happening. I felt that I couldn't stand it if I lost the baby."

The numbing effect of shock is the defense mechanism God built into our bodies to shield us from the "I can't stand it" trauma of severe pain. When you first learn that your baby has died, you aren't yet ready to deal with the overpowering feelings. The emotional paralysis provides time to absorb what has happened.

If there is warning of a miscarriage before the baby dies, as in my case, denial can start before you actually miscarry. We tend to believe that it couldn't happen, and we try to bargain with God. "If You'll only let my baby live, I'll . . ."

After Ann began spotting, her pregnancy lingered for six weeks. She hung in limbo, waiting and wondering.

"At first [after the miscarriage] I felt relief, because all along I had a feeling it was going to happen. Then I chastised myself for feeling relieved, because at the time I thought that meant I didn't want the baby. After sorting things out, though, I knew I did want it. I couldn't allow myself to get excited about having the baby, yet I couldn't prepare myself for a miscarriage because I felt that would be giving up hope. When I got over that, I could feel the loss."

Shock wanes, but only in tune with our capacity to experience those feelings of loss. It's different for each of us. Denial eventually turns to anger and pain, but not all at once. You may confront your tragedy for a while, and then find yourself mulling over a plan for the baby, forgetting that he isn't coming.

Trish told me about lying on the floor several days after her miscarriage at twelve weeks, trying to think of names for the baby. "All of a sudden I remembered there wasn't going to be a baby, and I just started to cry."

Flipping back and forth between disbelief and a desire to recount every detail, between crying and rigid control is OK. The death of your baby is a tough thing to accept, and you need time for it to sink in. When the pain starts, healing has begun.

PHYSICAL SYMPTOMS

When emotional feeling returns, a number of uncomfortable physical hurts may accompany it. It's common to feel completely exhausted, yet not be able to sleep, or to sleep constantly and never wake up refreshed. It isn't unusual to be plagued with nightmares about the baby and about death in general.

Your appetite may diminish because of the lump in your throat, or you may binge to try to fill the emptiness inside. You may feel faint, numb or nauseous. You may have a bout of diarrhea or vomiting.

Some women, and even some men, report a heaviness in their chest, butterflies in their stomach, frequent swallowing and heart palpitations. Many women have told me that their arms actually ached to hold their babies. After my D & C I felt cold, and my legs trembled uncontrollably. I asked the nurse over and over again if that was normal. It is normal for one in mourning, as is any kind of distress you may feel. Heartache is physical pain.

ANGER

When your emotions return, anger is usually one of the first that crashes in. You may feel anger toward your friends for not being supportive; anger at people who have children so effortlessly and don't seem to want them; anger at yourself and your powerlessness; anger at your spouse for not feeling the disappointment as deeply as you do; anger at the hospital staff for their lack of attention and care, for their failure to provide information, or their inability to save your baby. You may feel angry about the D & C, at having been poked and prodded and scraped and cleaned out like a piece of machinery. You may even feel anger at the baby — for no reason at all!

Feeling angry at God for letting this happen to you is common. Of course, as Christians, that kind of anger scares us because we're afraid He'll reject us for being mad at Him. Believe me, He can take it. He wants us to trust Him enough to be honest with Him. He knows how healthy anger can be.

A number of faithful people in the Bible knew anger: Moses, Job, the psalmists, the prophets, and even Jesus. But each one of them used anger as an energizer to help them fight self-pity and touch their true feelings.

If you've ever become angry with someone you love, you know that only after you clear the air can you hope to strengthen your relationship. It works that way with God, too. So shake your fist and tell Him how you feel! It's perfectly OK.

The danger of this powerful emotion lies in letting it go on for too long and taking it out in destructive ways. In their study at LaCrosse Lutheran Hospital, Rana Limbo and Sara Wheeler found that anger in many women increased from the time of their miscarriage until the projected due date.[2] Any anger that lingers longer than that probably bears some looking into. We'll look more at how to deal with anger in the next chapter, but for now, maybe you need to search for a constructive way to channel it. Scrub floors. Play the piano. Punch your fist into a pillow. Just don't deny it. Anger turned inward becomes chronic depression.

GUILT

A study done by Clemson University sociologists showed that mothers whose babies died after birth experienced anger and bitterness, while mothers who suffered miscarriage or stillbirth predominantly felt guilt.[3]

You may spend many weeks looking back over your pregnancy, seeking a cause for your loss in something you did. You may talk to people who reinforce your guilt with their lack of knowledge on the subject. "I told you that you shouldn't have waited so long to try to start your family," said a friend of Lynn's after her third miscarriage. That one sentence plunged Lynn into a downward spiral.

Miscarriage is not your fault. Yes, you were the baby's parents, but no parent can protect his child constantly.

Unfortunately, it is possible to feel guilty without *being* guilty. You can resolve true guilt by confessing sin, accepting forgiveness and changing your behavior. But if you aren't truly guilty, as in the case of a miscarriage, you can't resolve your feelings so simply, and they tend to drag on and on. Ask as many questions as you need to in order to assure yourself that nothing you could have done would have changed things. Talk it out, and let it go. Don't let it haunt you.

You may spend time agonizing over the mixed feelings you had about your baby when you first learned that you were pregnant. You may also feel guilty about letting other people down by grieving "too much" or for "too long." You might worry about the effect your grief is having on your family. You may think you should be able to recover from your loss within a few weeks.

Why not erase that word *should* from your vocabulary until you're well on the road to recovery? You have the right to feel what you feel. There are ways to help your family through the tough times, which we'll see later. But don't feel guilty because the road is rough or because it takes longer than you thought it would. It's God's healing process at work.

Finally, you might experience guilt over new doubts about the Lord that pop into your mind. Doubt, however, isn't something to feel guilty for. Doubt forces you to ask tough questions. When you have tough questions, you seek answers. You pray. You scour the Bible. You seek truth in the words of good people around you. You'll not only find answers, but you'll also focus your anger and get back the peace you so desperately want. In time, you'll "get right" with the Lord again.

FEAR

In *A Grief Observed*, C. S. Lewis wrote, "No one ever told me that grief felt so like fear."[4]

It's normal to be frightened in grief by specific fears or a general anxiety.

Touched for the first time by the reality of death, a mother may become terrified that other members of her family, particularly her other children, will die, too.

If a woman in her late thirties has experienced years of infertility before becoming pregnant, she may now be gripped with the fear that her failed pregnancy was her last chance.

Fears linked to your own situation will crop up. Linda was an only child, as was her father. After having one son, she miscarried. She feared that her son, too, was doomed to be an only child. She wanted a "family," and, to her, one child wasn't enough.

Perhaps you are afraid of trying to become pregnant again. Anyone who has been through a miscarriage is likely to fear that the nightmare will repeat itself and that pregnancy will always mean failure.

Maybe you're afraid of the intensity of your grief as I was. You're frightened of crying, fearing you won't stop and will lose your sanity. It crossed my mind several times that maybe I was going crazy.

I suffered what many grieving mothers experience: a panicky stage when the agony becomes almost intolerable. We can think of nothing else but the lost baby. We dream about him. We become absent-minded. I ran the washer through an entire cycle without putting in the clothes. More than once I forgot to pack Marijean's lunch to take to the babysitter.

Thinking muddles, and fears of entering a mental hospital plague us. But panic is normal. After the loss of a baby, we're confused and frightened by the nagging fear and continual inner questioning. Acute anxiety attacks and the waves of grief that sweep over us feel unfamiliar and horrifying. The feelings of being trapped and betrayed resemble feelings of paranoia.

But no matter how bad you feel, you aren't losing your mind. The bombardment of such strong emotions can disorient and depress you. That's normal for a person living through the death of someone they've loved.[5] You're dealing with the unknown, and we often fear what we don't understand.

The fear *will* fade, and you'll think rationally and feel hopeful again. It'll be OK.

SADNESS

Don't be frightened if your loss sends you reeling while your friends say, "It isn't like you to take things so hard." Suzanne told me that her husband, Jim, was confused over her despondence.

"We would go out to eat, and I would sit there and start crying. Jim would say, 'This is not Suzanne. Suzanne doesn't do this. Other women do this. Not Suzanne.'"

When it dawns on you how dreadful your loss really was, don't even try to be strong. Cry if you want to. Wail out all your agony. It may seem violent to you, but it's a healthy release. You won't lose control. When your body is ready to stop crying, your sobs will cease.

There may be certain times when the waves hit you more forcefully than others. I broke down while driving back and forth to work. Another woman, Missi, reports crying at mealtimes. Bedtime may be a vulnerable time for you. Whenever it happens, crying feels good. It hurts more not to.

Perhaps other Christians will tell you that you shouldn't feel sad, because your baby is better off where he is, with the Lord. But your sadness is really for yourself. You're empty and disappointed. Your hope of being a parent has been crushed. That's a legitimate sadness, and God feels it with you.

At first everything will be a reminder, and you'll feel a constant, oppressive sadness. Then your disappointment will come over you in waves that rise and subside in a rhythm. Go with them. Eventually they'll disappear, and you'll have peace.

INSTABILITY

About five days after my miscarriage I was sitting at a Christian writers' group meeting when suddenly I felt as if I would break down and go out of control. I grabbed the seat of my chair, terrified that I might jump up and scream or fall on the floor and cry. No one noticed me, and I didn't fly into a frenzy, but I was frightened.

I realize now how normal that experience was, particularly since I plunged back into activities so soon.

Whenever something unexpected and tragic happens to us, we are shaken by the reminder that nothing on earth is certain or permanent. Suddenly everything seems uncertain, and we feel vulnerable and out of control.

Jean shared a similar reaction: "I felt that my feelings were exposed, no matter how hard I tried to hide them. Many times it bothered me to be around people who knew what had happened, especially when the subject of babies or pregnancy came up. I would try to act normal and nonchalant but couldn't control the physical reactions. My throat tightened, and I'd feel like I had to swallow. My breathing became shallow. I would try to exit as quickly as possible without being too obvious. I didn't want to be pitied."

Those feelings can bring on a sense of failure and loss of self-esteem.

A few nights after my miscarriage, my father-in-law came to Dayton to spend some time with us, and because I was still having trouble sleeping, I stayed up late to chat with him.

"You know, Dad," I said, "family is a wonderful thing. No matter what you do, they still seem to accept you and stick by you."

His eyebrows shot up in surprise. "Honey, I hear failure in your voice," he said. "You don't have anything to be ashamed of. You haven't let anybody down. We all love you, and we're just concerned about you and Jim and Marijean."

I hadn't known until then how much of a failure I felt, and not until much later did I know how much I was like many other women who have been where I was.

"I was stripped of all pride and accomplishment," wrote Pam Vredevelt after losing her baby at five months. "Where other women had succeeded, I had failed."[6]

"I hate to fail at anything," Trish told me, "and my own body betrayed me!"

"Why had we called so many, so soon, about the pregnancy?"
Ann Kiemel Anderson wrote in *Taste of Tears — Touch of God*.
After years of infertility, and some corrective surgery, she finally
became pregnant but lost the baby at two months. "Now we
would have to let them all know it was over. I felt embarrassed.
There *was* something defective about me."[7]

When your body calls into question your ability to perform
a fundamental act, you stop trusting it. This damages your self-esteem, since a large part of your self-concept is tied to your body.
You started out on an important project, and it was literally
aborted. That feels like failure.

The danger in tying miscarriage to failure for too long is
that it can generalize into a feeling of overall worthlessness. You
may begin to feel that you can't accomplish anything, so why
try? Humiliating experiences from your past may choose now to
come back and nag you. I'd fought depression before, and soon
after William died, those old patterns threaded their way back
into my thoughts. I started to feel that I just couldn't cope.

The solution? Try to keep your loss in perspective. Tell
yourself that you've done nothing wrong. Accept your confusion
and vulnerability as part of your preoccupation with sadness, and
let it run its course. Don't be alarmed when almost anything
during this period — from a broken cookie jar to a phone that
won't stop ringing — topples your control. If you respond in an
unusually irritable manner and are oversensitive to slights from
other people, that's OK. Your coping mechanisms are being over-
taxed, so you're falling back on more primitive ways of dealing
with life. When you begin to regain your self-esteem (and you
will), things will right themselves again.

As Christians we can counteract feelings of failure as soon
as they creep in. We can remind ourselves that only God has the
power to control the outcome of every effort. Events that don't
unfold as we planned are not personal failures for us. God doesn't
want us to feel defeat.

ISOLATION AND EMPTINESS

Carl Sandburg once said, "A baby is God's opinion that the
world should go on."

When your baby dies, it seems that life isn't "going on,"
and the cloud of emptiness that descends can be smothering.
You see a barren womb in a sonogram. You leave the hospital
with no baby in your arms. You empty the dresser drawers in
the nursery. Where there were dreams and plans and hopes, now

there is nothing.

When you feel that emptiness, you feel it by yourself. Most of the people around you don't understand the support you need, so their well-meant consolation, "It could have been worse," isolates you still further.

Worst of all, you may feel abandoned by God, too. Through no fault of your own, you may feel that He has forgotten about you, or because you're depressed and can't readily accept what's happened, that you're not worthy of His love and care.

You may even purposefully shut people out of your life, preferring instead to be alone with your feelings. But being able to fool people with your stoic behavior only increases feelings of isolation. People *want* to believe you're doing well and, in your state of faltering self-esteem, you want them to believe it, too. So you smile and bravely straighten your shoulders, all the while dying inside.

You may close God out of your life as well. Because it seems arrogant to question Him, you may be tempted to brush off your loss with the justification that "it was God's will," and then find yourself no longer speaking to Him.

Feeling lonely and left out, you may notice the stirrings of jealousy. Many mothers who've recently experienced a loss find it hard to face their friends who are pregnant or who have infants, because they feel as if they themselves have been singled out "to lose." Carla, after four miscarriages and only one healthy baby, could barely stand to be around her sister-in-law, who was expecting a third, unplanned child. She was afraid her jealousy would erupt and ruin their relationship.

PREOCCUPATION

While trying to cope with loss, it's natural to become preoccupied with it. Over and over you recount what happened, to yourself and to anyone else who will listen. It's an attempt to make the loss real and to make some sense out of it. You might find it hard to settle back into a routine or to make even the simplest decisions. You may become overly dependent on your husband for a while. That's OK. It's part of grieving.

When a woman loses several pregnancies, the feelings of despair can be almost never-ending. A mother's obsession with blame and a growing self-hatred can take their toll on her and her family. With each loss, the grieving becomes more difficult because the mother's fear that she will never have a healthy child increases.

Carla's story of multiple loss is a heartbreaking one.

"After each one of my four miscarriages I felt more and more frustrated and frightened. I *had* to give Jim a child. What kind of wife would I be if I didn't? I had a very strong need to bear a child for myself, too. Because the doctors could give me no reasons for the failures, I felt at a real loss. Finally, after we were married nine years, I had Ryan. Now Ryan is four and I've just lost another one. It's been five months since my miscarriage, and I still feel terrible, even though I now have Ryan. Why can't I give my husband another child, and my son a sister or brother, and myself a baby?"

Double everything that's been said here if the loss of a pregnancy follows a history of infertility. Anyone who has had difficulty conceiving can tell you how painful and demoralizing it can be. The discovery that you're pregnant suddenly brings you into a club that you've been excluded from all your life, and the death of your baby abruptly puts you out of it once again, leaving you with a deep longing to belong. Once you've conceived and your baby dies, it's hard to accept your infertility and get on with things. Frustration and fear replace acceptance.

UP FROM GRIEF

Regardless of the magnitude of your loss, the grieving will end, no matter how endless it may seem now. You *will* feel better. Time helps, but that alone won't do it. There's "grief work" involved in recovery, which we'll cover in the next chapter.

In the meantime, don't do what I did.

Don't try to forget the baby — you never will. The scar will always exist. You'll think of your lost baby even after you have other children. You'll recall even the most minute details of your loss. As Nancy Berezin writes in *After a Loss in Pregnancy,* "The object is not to forget, but to remember . . . and go on."[8]

Don't immediately "count your blessings." For example, don't tell yourself, "I already have one healthy child," or, "It could have been worse." It could have — but you have *this* to deal with now. Belittling your grief only hides your true feelings and hinders your progress.

Don't try to reassure other people who acknowledge your loss. It's not your job now to take care of anyone else.[9]

Don't waste time worrying about what other people think of your grief. Remember that how you act outwardly is far less important than how you treat yourself inwardly.[10] The person who shows no feeling is probably suffering more than the one who expresses a lot. Give yourself permission to cry, talk and call forth what few memories there are. Ask for a hug when you need one. Be kind to yourself. Forgive yourself for your "negative" emotions. Don't fear for your sanity. Remember that you're a grieving person, and you have that right.

Above all, remember that even if you're angry with God, He won't let you "slip over the edge." Even for stubborn people like me who refuse to confront pain, He finds a way to pull them up from grief and enrich their lives through their loss. Your grief will soften. Hope will return. It will happen for you. I promise, and so does He.

EIGHT

How Do We
Get Better?

Pam Vredevelt is a professional counselor, and her husband is a pastor. When their baby died five months into her pregnancy, they knew what they would have to endure to recover from their loss. They felt as much pain as anyone else in their situation. They got just as depressed, cried just as hard, lost just as much sleep. But they always knew that peace lay ahead. They knew they would feel better; they knew they would heal, and they focused on what they had to do to make it happen.

GRIEF WORK

Not all of us are that fortunate. Many couples don't realize that it takes more than just time to get over the death of a baby. "Mourning," says Sara Bonnett Stein in her children's book, *About Dying*, "is not just feeling sad."[1] It's *work*; mental health professionals call it "grief work."

It's also painful work. It hurts to take those first steps toward recovery. It's hard to release feelings you invested in another or to let yourself be touched by the emotions that your loss unleashes. It takes energy to move through the hurt instead of looking for routes around it.

But working through grief is the way we recover. Such work reminds us that we aren't always going to feel as emotionally lousy as we do today. Our efforts signal to our Lord our willingness to heal and grow. If we sit, listlessly waiting for a better day, it simply doesn't come.

Grief work can be confusing. One minute you think that hurling yourself back into your old routine will help, and the next you're certain that all you have the desire or energy to do is lock yourself in a room and brood.

Actually, both of those activities have their proper place in your grief. Your real need is to strike a delicate balance between the two.

There will be times when you'll feel like wrestling with your anger and guilt and fear. Do it. There will be times when you'll want to throw yourself into cleaning out the refrigerator to rid yourself of tension. Do it. There will be times when you'll want to stare out the window and cry. Do that, too.

Just don't spend all your time dealing with your baby's death or all your time trying to get back to normal. Some of us have erred in both directions.

When I looked back in my journal to the weeks following my miscarriage, I noticed that after only one week of letting myself be sad, I pushed myself back into the world and insisted that I carry the same load of activities as before. For more than a year afterward, my life became one anxious attempt after another to "get on top of things." As you know, it didn't work.

Other women bog down in their endless recounting of the details of their loss. They worry about how they will ever go on, until sometimes they actually refuse to do so. I'm not judging anyone who falls into that trap. It's easy to do, and eventually anyone who feels she is drowning in sorrow will surface again. But finding a balance between grief and activity is God's goal for us.

The apostle Paul tells us that Christians don't grieve as others do. We always have hope (1 Thessalonians 4:13). As you heal from the pain of your baby's death remember that "God is at work within you, helping you want to obey him, and then helping you do what he wants" (Philippians 2:13, TLB). He'll be there for you as you take those painful steps.

Let's take a look now at the recovery process.

DEALING WITH YOUR GRIEF

"Love," says Bernadine Kreis in *Up From Grief*, "cannot

accept a death quickly."[2] Since acceptance must come eventually, though, it's helpful to relive your experience. Think about your loss. Take the time to be alone and silent, or to be together as a couple and mull over the details of your baby's death.

Your thoughts may automatically turn to that sad day. Whenever I crawled into bed and closed my eyes, I saw the bathtub filling with blood and Dr. Myer's face as he searched for the heartbeat. That kind of rumination may tear you apart, but it brings on healthy tears that help wash away the pain.

As you curl up in your favorite chair or take a walk, envision your baby and the life you planned to share with him. You'll cry, perhaps, but you'll also be able to say to yourself, "Hey, I lost someone *important!*" You'll start to accept your loss and understand why you feel so bad.

Talking is another therapeutic way to relive your loss and recover from pain. In the first few days after William died, the only time I really felt like myself was when I was recounting the details of our experience to people who cared about me and willingly listened. Jim nodded patiently as I told him over and over all the things that ran through my mind while we were in the emergency room. I found that breaking the news to people gave me a chance to talk and provided a release. Even after eighteen months passed and I needed to go back and resolve my grief, pouring my feelings out to caring people was comforting. There's something healing about releasing those pent-up memories.

There may be folks who won't want to discuss your loss at all or who will behave as if nothing happened. That's hard, and we'll address that in a later chapter. But know that there usually are people out there who will be willing to hear you out. Other women who've been through a miscarriage are often the best candidates. They know you need to talk, and they can make you feel less alone. If you don't know another miscarriage victim, seek out a support group. We'll look at how to find such a group later.

Don't feel ashamed of this compulsion to communicate when you're grieving. I sense that God intended us to need each other in this way.

So if other people don't bring up your loss, initiate the dialogue yourself. As minister Vincent Paris Fish put it, "As soon as possible, the person who mourns should seek the waters of comfort within the hearts and souls of fellow human beings."[3]

All sorts of other "grief work" can hasten your recovery. One night when I couldn't sleep, I wrote a letter to Dr. Myer, thanking him for his gentle treatment of Jim and me. Later I joined the church choir. I'd always loved to sing and being able to let out all my pain and my hope and my emotional energy in an acceptable way brought me closer to God and to myself.

The thing that helped me most was writing out my feelings in a daily journal. I'd done this for years, but now it was especially helpful. If you have never tried keeping a journal, now is a great time to begin. Buy a spiral notebook or treat yourself to a special diary. Write down everything that happened. Record your emotions and what you're learning about yourself and your husband. Take down how you feel about the Lord, your friends, your family. Write down all the things you can't say to anyone, but that are thrashing around inside. You have so few memories of Baby. Write them down so they'll always be there for you. Putting it all in black and white makes it much more real.

Being creative helps, too. If you have a flair for composition, write a poem or a story for your baby. If art is your niche, paint him a picture or portray your feelings in oils or watercolor. Stitch a memorial in counted cross stitch or needlepoint. Do you have a green thumb? Make a flower arrangement in your baby's honor or plant a tree to memorialize his short life.

Doing projects with your hands, even if you think you're all thumbs, is wonderfully healing. When I was struggling to come to terms with my loss, it was Halloween. I concocted a Care Bear outfit for Marijean and, without realizing it, my efforts soothed me. I learned that every little thing I did helped, whether it had anything to do with the baby or not.

If you feel anger, focus it where it belongs. Write a letter to God and tell Him that you don't think your loss was fair. In your journal, rake your doctor over the coals if you think he treated you carelessly.

If fear plagues you, write down all the things that frighten you. Many fears look less terrifying once they're on paper, and you may be able to dismiss them. Talk to someone who loves you about the fears you can't seem to shake. Find information that eases your mind or helps you make decisions that will control real fears. Pray for the Lord's comfort.

The funeral is one of our society's healthiest means of dealing with grief. However, when a baby dies before birth there is usually no such memorial. You just go home from the hospital, and that's it.

But grief can be intensified and prolonged when there is no formal mourning observance.[4] Many mourning parents are beginning to create rites and tangible mementos for themselves. The ideas that follow are merely suggestions; what's important is that you do whatever makes you feel healthier or closer to your baby or whatever meets the particular need you feel most strongly.

You can begin by giving your baby a name, perhaps one you picked out for him before the miscarriage. Use the name in conversations about the baby, especially with your other children. You'll probably find it easier to feel and accept the loss if you can call your child "Sara" or "John." As Jack Hayford said in his excellent sermon, "Short-Circuited Into Eternity," naming the unborn child gives you a sense of his being.[5]

We selected the name William Bradley for our first boy, even before Marijean was born. I can't think of the baby we lost as anyone else, yet it's only been recently that I've referred to him by name when talking to others.

It takes courage to acknowledge your lost baby as a person when others think of him as an undifferentiated mass of tissue. But more and more parents, like Kathy and Rick Johnson, are realizing how much meaning this simple step can have.

After losing four babies, the Johnsons and their two sons went back and named each lost child and assigned a sex, an anniversary of death and an approximate birth date to each. Now each lost baby — Keith, Sara, Julia and Ryan — have a history of sorts which, Kathy says, gives substance to their losses and a stamp of legitimacy to the pain they've suffered as a family. They had none of that until they named them.

Jack Hayford also suggests that we present the child to the Lord, just as the parents do at the funeral of a child who was born and then dies. We carried the baby for a while. Now we must let God take over His care. Even years after the loss occurs, some formal means of letting go is helpful.

When I faced my need to suffer the death of William Bradley, I sat down one day with the *Book of Common Prayer* and read through the funeral service, supplying my own words to the Lord when I felt them rising in me. No one knelt beside me (although now I wish that I had shared the experience with Jim), and no one brought over a covered casserole afterward. But I was deeply moved by the sense of acceptance I felt when I closed the book. One prayer in particular touched me and helped me say good-bye:

> "O God, whose beloved Son took children into His arms and blessed them: Give us grace to entrust William Bradley to your never-failing care and love, and bring us all to Your heavenly kingdom; through Jesus Christ our Lord, who lives and reigns with You and the Holy Spirit, one God, now and

forever. Amen."

It is also helpful to create a physical memorial to your lost child. Contribute to a special cause for children. Let your other children take part, especially in remembering anniversary dates. Even a birthday cake isn't inappropriate.

Paula wears a cross for the baby she lost. "When I realized that no one but me is going to remember or care in twenty years," she says, "I knew I needed to make the baby substantial in *my* mind."

Ellen and Dick framed a print of their first ultrasound, taken when their baby son still fluttered happily in the womb. It stands next to their ten-year-old daughter's photo in a place of honor.

I wrote a letter to William, telling him of all the plans and dreams I had for him. I explained how I had intended to teach him to be sensitive and to feel free to cry and to take as much pleasure in making a pizza as in throwing a football.

I told him how much I longed to sit by our fireplace and rock him to sleep while Marijean sang the songs she and I had always shared. I wrote about how much I'd looked forward to hearing the two of them fight over the last piece of chocolate cake and discuss what girls like in a guy when they turned teenagers.

I assured him of our love and told him how much happier he would be with his heavenly Father. I tucked the letter into a box with a hat and booties someone knitted for him and put it away in a drawer. I don't look at it often, but I know it's there.

I can't emphasize this enough: Even though years may have passed since the death of your baby, if the facts and feelings were never faced, it's not too late. Other people may say, "Oh, for heaven's sake! You're still grieving over that?" Don't let them intimidate you. You're doing what's best for yourself, and you're doing the grieving work God wants you to do. It feels good to finally be honest with yourself and stop pretending!

TAKING YOUR MIND OFF YOUR PAIN

Although dealing with your pain is vital to recovery, from the beginning you'll need some enjoyable distractions to help you think about something else. Slowly these activities do become more and more enjoyable, and you will need less time to grieve.

But that first small step is the hardest. The following activities and ideas might make your readjustment process easier:

Be nice to yourself. Give yourself hugs in as many ways as possible. Treat yourself the way you wish other people would treat you right now.

Cling to the security of home and family if you want to. Ask for time to snuggle with your husband. Hold your other little ones on your lap. Call your sister long-distance and tell her you love her.

Examine your routine, and change its stressful activities if you can. That may mean getting up a little earlier so you don't awaken to the hassles of forgotten lunches and lost math books. It may mean calling a halt to all chores after dinner and spending the time reading the Bible or leafing through a magazine instead. If the task of cooking meals threatens to overtake you, let it be order-in pizza or a trip to Arby's. Slow your pace, because dealing with grief exerts enough pressure.

Expect that at first nothing will seem like much fun. Even things you once loved to do will seem like stale pleasures. But as your pain lessens, your interest will sparkle again. Help it. Plan things you can look forward to. Forego dusting for a day, and take your kids on an impromptu picnic. Plan to windowshop after work, and meet your husband for pie and coffee. You won't be ready for big events for a while, but the little things can mean a great deal.

Most of all, be patient with yourself. Believe me, your recovery isn't going to happen overnight! You want others to give you time, so you give yourself time. And give yourself love. When I gave in to my need to grieve, I folded my arms across my chest, cried, and stroked my own sleeves. It's a comforting habit I still fall into when life gets tough.

Take care of yourself physically, too. That's essential to anyone's grief work, but especially for you since you're recovering from pregnancy as well. Battered by the abrupt shift in your hormones, you probably feel exhausted. Help yourself regain some of that physical vitality.

A good diet is a must. Your doctor or a good book on nutrition can help you. If at first the thought of eating does not excite you, munch on whatever you think you can get down or that appeals to you, but try not to skip meals. You may exist on Snickers and club soda for a few days, but as soon as you regain some of your appetite, get on a good diet and stay on it. It *will* help you feel better; not eating properly will only slow your recovery.

Take it easy physically. Get plenty of rest those first few weeks, and get off your feet when fatigue sinks in. When you're tired, it's more difficult to cope with negative feelings, and there's no reason to make your recovery more trying than necessary.

Often, painful memories will rob you of sleep. Medication usually isn't a good idea unless your bouts with insomnia are prolonged. A hot cup of chamomile tea, a relaxing bath, or a snack of turkey and cheese can help you drift off. I grew to love warm milk served in a crystal goblet.

If you don't sleep well at night but nod off during the day, try to arrange your schedule so that you can nap in the afternoon until you get back to normal. Don't browbeat yourself for tossing and turning; rest as much as you're able.

Exercise can help you relax, as well as make you hungry and bring on sleep. Mental health professionals have known for some time that exercise helps stabilize moods. Before you start, or resume, an exercise plan, though, check with your doctor and get his OK.

If you've resisted exercise in the past and have never been a whiz at sports, be creative. Ride your bicycle every afternoon with your toddler strapped in a carrier behind you. Take walks at sunset with your husband. Get an exercise tape, record or video that you can fit into your schedule. If it would help to buy some cute tights and a leotard, do it.

If you want to get more serious about exercising, join a health club or participate in free exercise classes. Jogging is an inexpensive sport that you can pursue anytime, anywhere. There are many excellent books available to guide you. Helpful literature exists for virtually any physical activity you'd like to pursue.

Be sure that any fitness plan helps you relax, cope and feel better about yourself. It shouldn't compound your stress. I took up a serious running plan in my effort to get back on an even keel but ended up making it a competitive activity. That wasn't what I needed then, but I'm still proud that I finished a half-marathon.

Now I've settled into thirty minutes of running three times a week. I also do aerobics on alternate days and ride a ten-speed bike whenever I'm in the mood. This plan rekindled a love and appreciation for my body without making exercise a have-to.

To take the best care of your body after a miscarriage, avoid the use of drugs and alcohol. Any medication should be taken only under the supervision of your physician. Many seemingly innocent substances are addictive and can lead to chemical dependence. They may also stop or delay the necessary grieving process.

Other people may tell you to resume your normal activities

as quickly as possible and, in part, that's good advice. Returning to those things that raise your self-esteem is an excellent idea, but do it only when you feel ready. Give yourself time to grieve before you force yourself to go back to work, take up your church commitments or even clean the oven. Be sure you aren't flying into the household or office routine so that you can "forget."

At first you might follow Barbara Berg's advice in *Nothing to Cry About.* She advises that you try to do a little more each day of something that has nothing to do with the baby or the pregnancy.[6]

If you work at home, your housekeeping doesn't have to be immaculate, but doing the essentials will make you feel useful, and that's a start. If you work at an outside job, just showing up for work and making it through the day might be an accomplishment.

Little by little you'll start to rebuild your store of energy and enjoyment of life. As you realize that your other children still come to you to have their shoes tied and their tears dried, as you see that your co-workers still seek your advice, as you find your friends dropping by for coffee and a sympathetic ear from *you,* your good feelings about your own worth will return.

HURDLES AND TROUBLE SPOTS

Some parts of recovery are harder than others. There are some that you can't run from. When you do face them, you're that much closer to recovery. The following places and activities will be some of the most painful reminders of your loss:

- the nursery full of crying newborns during your hospital stay;
- your post-D & C checkup;
- chance encounters with pregnant women, babies and nursing mothers;
- get-togethers with relatives who are pregnant or who have just given birth; and
- the act of putting away your maternity clothes and baby things.

There are other painful reminders that eventually you'll learn to live with, but that for now you should try to avoid. The list is unique to every mother, but here are a few of the most common, and torturous reminders:

- baby showers (send a gift and a warm note — your friends will understand);
- the grocery store's baby supplies aisle (skip it);
- maternity stores (slip by the window);
- Pampers and Playtex nursers commercials (change the channel — quickly); and
- discussions with friends about babies and pregnancy (discreetly excuse yourself or switch the conversation to the sale at Macy's).

SIGNS OF HEALING

Signs that healing is occurring are easily recognized. They feel a lot like relief.

One day, you'll realize that several hours or perhaps even a whole day passed and you didn't think of the baby or your sadness at all.

You'll realize with a start that you're singing in the shower, or that you just laughed without having to prompt yourself with, "OK, that was supposed to be funny. Laugh, you fool."

You'll wake up one morning wanting to get to your desk, or feeling eager to plan your six-year-old's birthday party, rather than sighing and saying, "Today I have to get this done." Your old interests will reawaken, all by themselves.

Spontaneously you'll count the blessings you do enjoy. You won't be forcing yourself to "look at the bright side." You'll be truly thankful, as I am when I look into Marijean's chocolate-fudge brown eyes and praise God that I didn't miss those, too.

You'll find yourself treasuring what's yours, possibly more than you would have otherwise. "I appreciate every child now," says Anne, who suffered nine miscarriages. "Every one is special."

In spite of how you felt a few months before, you'll discover that you're looking forward to the future and making plans: maybe for another pregnancy, perhaps for an adoption, or possibly for something that has nothing to do with babies at all.

In true recovery, life will no longer be one long, desperate attempt to cover your grief. The joy of life will re-emerge, and you will recognize it. St. Augustine said that after grief, time plants in us other hopes and memories, and little by little they fill us up again with our "former sources of delight."[7] Your healthy pain will at last bring its own healing.

LETTING GO

When that happens, it's time to let go of your grief. Even

though you'll be so glad to feel like a human being again, letting go and getting on with your life can sometimes be hard.

After all, your anguish is your only tie to your baby, and you may feel downright guilty leaving it behind. You may wonder if it is a slight to him that you can live peacefully without him in your arms.

Letting go is part of being a mother. It doesn't imply a lack of love, nor does it mean that, in accepting his death, you're forgetting your baby. You just don't have to hurt for him anymore.

How do you let go?

You admit that there are some things in this life that are simply out of your control. You say to yourself, "I've found out everything I can. I've shared it all with the people I love. I've allowed myself to feel everything I feel. Now the responsibility for it goes to the Lord. I'm going on."

In psychological terms, that's called *closure*, a formal ending to a particular situation. Closure comes differently for everyone, so I can tell you only how it happened for me and hope that you will find your own path to grief's end.

Twenty-three months had elapsed since William Bradley's death. After hiding from my grief for a year and a half, I'd spent the last several months struggling with all the heartache I was afraid and ashamed to face before.

And it was happening; I was recovering. But I still hadn't "let go" of the baby and the sadness that surrounded him.

Barb, a close friend, guided me through the steps of closure. One Saturday a few weeks before Christmas, she took me to Reno to do some Christmas shopping. At mid-afternoon snow began to fall, so we hurried into a Marie Callender's restaurant for lunch.

I sat at a table, snuggled cozily into a bay window seat, with a steaming bowl of potato soup and a mound of sourdough bread in front of me. Outside, snow converted the Nevada streets into a sparkling showplace. Suddenly I looked across the food with its rising steam and, as I listened to Barb's cheerful banter, I started to cry happy, grateful tears.

"I have it all," I told her. "I have beauty and warmth and love and God in my life. What more do I need?"

And I meant it. I had let go.

How long will that take for you? Don't measure what's normal for you by how long it takes someone else to recover. Missi says it was a good three months before she could "look back and think objectively about it." For Ann, it took more than a year. Because of my circuitous course, it took me nearly two years.

RECOVERY TIME

In their study at LaCrosse Hospital, nurses Sara Wheeler and Rana Limbo found that most women were fully recovered from anywhere between six weeks after their miscarriage to the date originally set for delivery of the baby.[8]

In her book *The Other Side of Pregnancy*, Sherry Jiminez writes that by six weeks after their loss, most women are back to some sort of routine. At six months most are able to see growth in themselves and even understand their friends' reactions.[9]

Several factors influence the length of your healing process:

● your past experiences (I was so frightened by the likeness of my grief to my previous bouts with depression that I was convinced I was a "mental case." I felt I must recover quickly to prove to myself that I wasn't a lost cause.);

● other losses in your life;

● how you felt about your pregnancy;

● how abruptly the miscarriage interrupted your pregnancy;

● how your family expresses grief (My mother experienced the death of her mother, son and husband all within ten years, yet her response — even around my sister and me — was stoic. I know now that she grieved privately, but the message to me was that I should accept life's tragedies and move on.);

● how you usually handle your feelings;

● how much support you receive from others, especially from your spouse;

● other stresses present in your life and the success you're having in handling them;

● your physical condition; and

● the options open to you for having more children.

However, certain facets of the healing process are true for everyone:

(1) *The healing process is slow.* It always takes longer than you thought it would, and you can't hurry it. That would be as senseless as attempting to speed up recovery from major surgery.

(2) *There are no shortcuts.* You have to feel and work through everything.

(3) *Even after you think it's over, setbacks will occur.* I cried along with Maureen on *The Guiding Light* when she had her miscarriage. I sobbed into Jim's chest when his sister Penny

gave birth to a 9-pound boy. When the Christmas season approaches, I feel an occasional twinge because I'm not buying Tonka trucks for my small son.

If dark times come to you again, it's OK. In fact, expect them, because the love in your heart hasn't died.

If you've been on a steady diet of grief for many months with virtually no change and there is no relief in sight, don't be afraid to get professional help. Perhaps a family counselor or psychologist would be helpful to you, or maybe you'd prefer meeting with a clergyman who is experienced in counseling grief victims. Don't be ashamed to take such a step. God plants these people in our lives to assist us in putting the pieces of life back together. For signals that you're in need of special assistance, see Appendix IV.

As long as you *want* to recover, you will. As you'll see in the chapters ahead, the person you are becoming in the process is someone who is wiser, stronger and richer in the Holy Spirit. That's a goal worth working toward.

NINE

Not Just Healing, But Growing

Once I finally set about the task of grieving, I was frightened by the torrent of doubts about God that hit me.

What kind of God are You if You give, just to take away? I asked. *Do You do whatever You feel like doing, on mere whim? Am I just some toy of Yours? Or should I have been a better person? Prayed harder, maybe? Am I supposed to go on loving You and respecting You and — ha! — trusting You after what You've done? God . . . are You sure You're even THERE?*

Flinging those questions at a God whose decisions I'd always accepted without question was disconcerting.

DOUBTS

It helped when I learned that I wasn't the first miscarriage victim who suffered from doubt. An excerpt from a responsive reading written by Janis Heil of UNITE, a support group in Philadelphia, sums up what many parents feel after the death of their baby: "Some people tell us it was Your will; that it was for the best; that You needed an angel in heaven. They say, 'God doesn't give us more than we can handle.' I don't believe any of it. My faith is sorely tested. I found myself doubting Your love and even Your existence."

The questions for God don't always come to our minds right away. Some of us turn immediately to the Lord for comfort when the baby dies, and only later do we turn *on* Him with a vengeance.

"At first I could accept that the Lord had it all under control," said Ellen. "Twenty-four hours later doubts and depression rushed in."

Once the shock and denial dissolve and the full force of the tragedy strikes, it's human to question God, and it's also OK with Him. If you look back at the questions I hurled heavenward, you'll see that they show several things about me:

● I believe God exists.
● I believe He knew what happened in my life and how I felt about it.
● I believe He had control over it.
● I believe He cared enough to listen to me.[1]

Sometimes despair marks the beginning of a real understanding of God. For some of us it's only after we've wrestled with our questions and doubts and shouted them at God that we can hear His response. Perhaps it's only through resisting His way and trying to find our own that we can come back, tail between our legs, and say, "OK, You really do know better than I do."

Sometimes when doubts crop up, we grow nervous and say, "This doesn't have anything to do with God." So we shove our questions away where they only fester and give rise to more pain later on. As is the case with most painful emotions, now is the time to face them.

But asking those questions fairly isn't always easy. For example, we risk expressing our angry demands in the wrong way. It's expected that we might make irrational statements. Just as He did with Job, God hears them but doesn't judge us for them.[2] It's quite another matter to curse Him. Complain and question, if you must, but beware of anger that turns you away looking for a better God.

CHOICES

Pat enlisted the help of a kind clergyman after she suffered her second miscarriage. For several months he listened to her struggles and watched her stomp impatient feet before he said, "You have to make a decision: Either you believe God loves you, or you believe He's out to get you." Of course, says Pat, there was really no choice. She settled the question and moved on.

Ann Kiemel Anderson also talks about choice after the death of her long-awaited baby. "There was a choice," she writes, "to make sorrow my friend or my enemy. To walk with it and let it teach me, or scorn it and become bitter."[3]

You must ask yourself, "Am I going to open myself to God's answers to these relentless questions, or am I going to shrug Him off and look elsewhere?"

Once you decide, the road to recovery is still not easy, but there are steps you can take to revitalize your relationship with God.
(1) *Go to God and say, "Help. I can't do this alone. I need Your comfort, or I won't make it."*

When at last I grieved William Bradley's death, it was the first time I ever looked to God and said, "Just hold me. I'm tired of trying to be wonderful. I need *You.*"

That's surrender. Not resignation, which says, "I can't do anything about it anyway, so take it, God." Not self-effacement, which says, "I'm too stupid (or weak or sinful or ugly) to deal with this." It's surrender: "I'm putting myself and my grief into Your hands because I know You'll walk through it with me."

There's awesome power in such a response. When I turned my grief over to the Lord (I used to wince when I heard people use that phrase. I didn't know what in the world they meant by it!) the pieces of my burden started falling away. St. Francis de Sales said that either God shields you from suffering or He gives you the unfailing strength to bear it.[4] Either way you really come to know your God.

None of this means that as soon as you turn your questions over to God you give up the struggle for recovery. You continue to seek answers to your questions, but you do it with Him at your side. *Together* you work it out.
(2) *Pursue an active, full-time partnership with God.*

I never knew what a conscious effort it took to put Christ first in every area of my life, because I had only a token relationship with Him before the miscarriage.

Many people have only a crisis relationship with God. They turn to Him when they are in desperate need, and not before.[5] Such a friendship among adults would be considered shallow and insufficient to meet heart-felt needs, and so it is with God. If you find yourself turning to God only when the traumas of life seem about to overwhelm you, you will want to consider enriching the spiritual flavor of your life by getting to know God better. (We'll look at ways to do this in a minute.) As you become better acquainted with Him and trust Him more, I encourage you to release more and more of yourself to Him. Like any friendship, the warmth of commitment and caring that will grow between you will form the basis of what can be the most meaningful, long-lasting relationship of your life.

Some people have no relationship with God at all. But in my opinion, there's no time like the aftermath of losing a baby to start one.

How can you enrich your relationship with God? Try these ideas:

• Set aside a special time each day just to be alone with God.

Don't let anything less than a major earthquake interfere with that time. Commune with God in ways that are meaningful to you. I sense a special nearness to Christ when I receive communion (a sacrament that reviews Christ's sacrifice of His body and blood). In His presence I can *really* pray. For Jim, God's touch comes through nature. He talks to God when he runs or climbs a mountain.

• Tell God how you hurt and what you're struggling with.

Perhaps you need to say, as Kathy did after her fourth miscarriage, "God, did You forget me? Lose my address? I'm doing all this nice Christian stuff! Where are You?"

Or say, as eventually I did, "Father, I can't sleep, and I can't eat, and I can barely function because I'm so tied up in knots. I don't want to live this way. I want to find peace. Please, be there even though I'm doubting You."

• Don't demand miracles.

We can only ask that God help us bear the struggles, answer the questions, lead us down the right path and give us the patience to wait for Him to work in His own time. It's so hard to give up that control!

Be certain, too, that you don't ask the same questions over and over. The question, Why, God? repeated for six months will get you nowhere. I love Nancy Berezin's analogy in *After a Loss in Pregnancy.* She says that when we badger God with the same questions like little children so often badger their parents, it shows that we don't really want to know the answers. We just want God to get sick of our nagging and give the baby back!

• Try not to bargain with God in your prayers.

Anne confesses that she tried to make deals when the bleeding started during each of her miscarriages. "But they were bargains I never could have kept," she says. Besides, God doesn't work "deals." When we make rash promises — "I vow to tithe if You'll wipe away this pain" — we bring God down to our level rather than rising to His in submission and humility.

● Saturate yourself with the Scriptures.

The Bible never had as much meaning for me as it did when I read it in the light of my fears and questions. Passages I'd read a hundred times spoke to me as if they'd just been translated from some foreign tongue, and I started to take massive doses of them.

Sitting down with the Bible before anyone else got up became a ritual with me. I read and re-read verses and even laughed out loud because the words were so perfect for my situation. I dashed mad notes in the margins. Those eventually spilled over into a notebook that I call My Spiritual Journal. Of course, I'm a compulsive writer, but the point is, I was absorbing His perspective on my problems, and that is the key.

The passages listed at the end of this chapter were helpful to me and to others. You might want to give them a try.

INSIGHTS

One of the biggest questions the Bible answered for me was this one: Where is my baby now? I was concerned for his soul, and although I knew God doesn't create life merely to destroy it, I needed concrete proof.

With the guidance of Jack Hayford in his tape, "Short-Circuited Into Eternity," I got the answers I needed through Bible verses like these:

> Psalm 22:10: Upon Thee I was cast from birth; Thou hast been my God from my mothers womb.

My insight: If God took care of my baby in the womb, surely He takes care of him now.

> Jeremiah 1:5: Before I formed you in the womb I knew you, and before you were born I consecrated you . . . (see also Isaiah 49:5)

My insight: Before these men emerged from the womb, God had ordained them for His work. Therefore, God has plans for my baby and is carrying them out.

> Ecclesiastes 6:3-5: If a man fathers a hundred children and lives many years, however many they be, but his soul is not satisfied with good things, and he does not even have a proper burial, then I say, "Better the miscarriage than

he, for it comes in futility and goes into obscurity; and its
name is covered in obscurity. It never sees the sun and it
never knows anything; it is better off than he."

My insight: An untimely birth is better than a rich man
whose soul is filled with evil. Not only was God taking care of
William in his death, but our little son is better off than we are.
He will skip root canals, broken hearts and grieving for lost
children. He will always be holy and never fall to the temptations
of life on earth that might have deprived him of salvation.

> 1 Corinthians 15:40: There are also heavenly bodies and
> earthly bodies, but the glory of the heavenly is one, and
> the glory of the earthly is another.

My insight: Earthly bodies and heavenly bodies are very
different things. For his earthly life our son had a body adequate
to his needs while he was beginning the process of becoming
what God wanted him to be. But I'm not going to have a
2-inch-long fetus to hold when I die. Someday I will know and
love my son's soul.

MISCONCEPTIONS

As we get to know God and acquaint ourselves with His
perspective on our situation through His Word and through prayer,
we must be careful not to misconstrue His words to us. There
are five common misconceptions that women in our position are
likely to have. (As I'm sure you'll believe by now, I had almost
all of them.)

Misconception #1: *Your miscarriage happened because God
wanted to teach you something or build your character.*

Jesus says that He prunes every branch that bears fruit to
make it bear even more (John 15:2). Some people, I think, misin-
terpret His promise. I don't believe that the God I love said, "I'm
going to give Nancy Rue a baby, and then I'm going to snatch
it away from her, just so she'll seek out a closer relationship
with Me (or get to know herself better or stop trying to be a
superwoman)."

The struggle through grief *can* help us grow, and with God's
help it does, but nothing in the Bible tells us that we should be
glad we're suffering.

Misconception #2: *You're more deserving of a child than
"that couple over there."*

I really wanted a son, and Jim would've been such a good dad to a little boy. We would have raised him to be a fine young man. Yet as a high school teacher I saw adolescents in my classroom every day who were once only unwanted teenage pregnancies to their parents. Their folks neglected them, abused them, over-indulged them and let them grow toward being unhappy adults. I was incensed. I knew we would've done a better job and I wondered why God wouldn't entrust another child to us.

God doesn't compare your life to someone else's, and neither should you. A phrase from Jacob Philip Rudin's essay, "Thoughts on My Wife's Death," turned my perspective on this point. "God must not be reduced to a cosmic bookkeeper," he said. "He isn't in the business of measurement or comparison of reward with reward, blessing with blessing."[6]

The most important way that you know God loves you is that He gave His Son's life for you. You can't adequately measure His love by the individual circumstances of your life.

Misconception #3: *Right away you should be ready to say, "It was God's will."*

In the end it is healthy to accept your baby's death as part of God's plan. But you may not be able to do so right away. If you do, you may also find yourself saying, "If it is God's will, what right do I have to grieve?" First confront your anger with God (and everybody else), and then make peace with His will.

Misconception #4: *Your faith should make grieving easy.*

Faith gives purpose to grief. But the myth that faith is an insurance policy against grief is just that: a myth. Jesus grieved over the deaths of John the Baptist and Lazarus. Your love for Christ and His love for you doesn't mean you get to waive pain. "He mourned the children He loved," wrote Ira Tanner in *The Gift of Grief.* "He expects you will mourn the loss of yours."[7]

I said to God, "You promised me comfort. Where is it? I want it now!" God said (as I often do to Marijean), "It's coming. It's coming. Be patient."

Misconception #5: *You should buy into the image of lost-baby-turned-angel.*

When Jean told me she imagined her lost baby as a little angel in heaven, I was touched, but that wasn't a mental picture I could form. Actually, I didn't want an angel in heaven. I wanted a baby in my arms, and so do a lot of other bereaved moms and dads. However, the image that did comfort me and that helped me was that of picturing my baby cradled in God's loving arms.

Seek a personal perspective on your tragedy that satisfies *you.*

GROWTH

You can emerge from the pit of doubts and questions and find that you have not only recovered from your pain, but also that you have grown into a new person — you will have outdistanced "your old self."

Yes, you have scars. A holiday never passes when I don't think how much William would have enjoyed the turkey or the fireworks or the trick-or-treating. Women tell me that they wonder, *Would six children have been much more work than five? How would my life have been different?*

But the scars you bear make you wise. They remind you to treat yourself and others with a new tenderness, an unaccustomed compassion. They poke you in the ribs when you forget to forgive people for their thoughtless remarks.

You can be serene because you've undergone the ultimate test of grief and not only have survived but also have found new strength. You have that peace that passes all understanding, that peace that comes even when all is not well.

I learned that I'm no less a woman because I couldn't carry my baby to term. Rather, I'm more of one because I sensitively mourned my child's death.

I know what's important now. It isn't being perfect. It isn't conquering the world. It's family.

I have come to appreciate what I have. Like Anne, who says she has nine dead babies but three living miracles, I look at Marijean as a marvelous creation. I drink in those soft brown eyes and watch the way her brow puckers when she concentrates. I listen to the way her voice changes octaves when she's pretending in her room. I don't say, "Not right now," quite as often. And every day I tell her how much I love her.

I don't take anything for granted, whether it's the way the Nevada sky turns maroon and silver on a summer evening or the fact that Jim comes home from work every night at 6 o'clock.

I listen to other people more intently, because I know now that God speaks through them.

I make decisions more carefully, weighing how my choices will affect others, but basing my final decision on what I feel is best and on what I think God wants.

The most fulfilling part of growth through grief can be a new relationship with the Lord. Kathy told me a story which I think sums up this possibility beautifully.

"In my quiet time one day, I said, 'Oh, God, it's not that I don't know where these babies are. I know they're with You. But

I can't live with the fact that they're not going to grow up in my home, that they won't sit at my table, that they won't crawl under the pew on Sunday mornings at my feet.' And God showed me the neatest thing — that He goes through the same thing. There are people in the world who don't know Him as their Father, and who don't sit at His table. He can't raise them in His house because they don't even know that He is their Father. That was a sweet, precious lesson for me. He seemed to be saying, 'We have something in common. We're in this together.'"

Now, there's no doubt in my mind that God is instrumental in every tiny part of my life, and I turn to Him for everything.

I'm not afraid of Him anymore.

I see death the way He does — not as an end but as a beginning — so I'm not afraid of death anymore, *or* of life.

I'm at peace with Him. I feel much less guilt, and I have quit my endless searching for the reasons for my behavior. I realize He doesn't owe me any explanations. Rather, I owe Him my trust. After all, if I understood everything, faith wouldn't be necessary.

Through my baby's death, I've found a new life. That isn't *why* William died, and I'm still not happy about it. If the miscarriage hadn't happened, God would have led me to Himself some other way. But if it had to be, I'm grateful that those hours of lonely suffering brought me to where I am right now.

I pray that for you, too. Whether you see your miscarriage as a reason for grief or view it as a sign to move on to the next life experience, it is a chance for you to learn and grow and to be all that the Lord wants you to be.

HELPFUL SCRIPTURE PASSAGES

Job 1:21; 2:10; 3:11-19
Psalm 22:9,10; 23; 27:1,3,5,7,13; 30; 32:8; 91:14-16; 113:7-9; 121; 138:8; 139
Proverbs 23:18
Ecclesiastes 3:1-8
Isaiah 25:8; 40:31; 43:2-5; 49:1,5a,16; 66:10
Jeremiah 31:13,14
Matthew 11:28-30; 18:1-6; 19:13-15
Mark 10:13-16
Luke 9:46-48; 18:15-17; 24:5
John 5:25,26; 6:51; 10:10; 11:21-27; 14:2,18,25
Romans 5:1-5; 8:28-39
1 Corinthians 15:51-58

2 Corinthians 7:9-11; 12:9,10
Philippians 4:7-9,13
Colossians 3:1-4
1 Thessalonians 4:13-18
Hebrews 6:10
1 Peter 5:7
Revelation 7:16,17

PART FOUR

Are We Alone?

For I am utterly helpless,
without any hope. One
should be kind to a
fainting friend, but you have
accused me without the
slightest fear of God.
    Job 6:13,14 (TLB)

TEN

Do Dads Hurt, Too?

When I returned from the recovery room on the night of my miscarriage, Jim put a weary head down on my bed, and I stroked his hair. That was the last sign of grief I saw in him for nearly two years.

I knew he was dealing with the loss. A roll of paper towels lay by the bed when I returned home the next day — a sure sign he'd been crying and blowing his nose. Immediately he began to tear apart our garage and, within a few months, turned it into a magnificent family room. I suspected that was part of his grief work.

But I never knew that he cried over William's death every day for two weeks until one morning twenty-two months later, or that he pulled over to the side of the road on the way home from the hospital the night of the miscarriage and sat for a long time, sorting out his feelings.

Most of his focus seemed to be on me, on how I was coping with my grief, on keeping me busy, on helping me look to the future. While he was comforting and understanding, his apparent lack of emotion made me suspect he didn't care about the baby. He can cry when he hears "The Star Spangled Banner"

90

played and turn crimson when the Forty-Niners lose. So since I saw him express no feelings over the death of William Bradley, I assumed he had none.

I never mentioned that disappointment to him, and very quickly the loss became mine rather than ours. A distance developed, and, without our realizing it, grew until it seemed like a chasm between us.

We started out being good communicators, but somehow our ability to really talk to each other disappeared over the years. Maybe Marijean's birth had something to do with it. Perhaps it came with the changes we were making as growing individuals. Possibly it was the result of a lack of self-confidence in both of us. We couldn't talk about money, sex or religion, and we certainly couldn't talk about something as personal as our pain. By the time we realized the mistake we'd made by not sharing our feelings, our marriage was in deep trouble.

That's quite common, but such distance between a husband and wife isn't inevitable. Going through an experience like a miscarriage can bring a couple closer together, as Pam Vredevelt points out in *Empty Arms.* "We are now more in love as husband and wife than ever before," she writes. "The pressure of grief cemented our previous romance into a magnificent ongoing love affair."[1]

Pam was not just lucky. Most any marriage can survive the hurt of miscarriage and come out healthier than it was before, but it isn't easy. It takes the use of grieving skills that may not yet have been developed because the loss of a baby may be the first tragedy the couple has experienced together.

Let's look first at steps you, as the wife, can take to protect your marriage while you grieve. Then we'll consider helpful tips for the husband, and then advice for both as you seek to turn this tragedy into a tool that will improve your relationship.

FOR WIVES

Several years ago, Erma Bombeck wrote a television series about a couple named Maggie and Len.

One evening Maggie and Len got into one of those "You-always-you-never" conversations, and Len, feeling uncomfortable, began to make jokes.

"That's just what you did when I had my miscarriage," Maggie told him. "I wanted that baby so bad, but when you came to the hospital, you just made jokes and tried to cheer me up. Not once did you cry with me. I didn't like you for a long time after that."

Len explained, rather tearfully, that he went home from the hospital that night, still playing the role of the staunch male, and went into the nursery to put away the paint cans and brushes. Then he carried the baby basket, still wet with fresh paint, up to the attic.

"I was doing fine," he said, "until I looked over and saw the little potty chair. That's when I sat down and cried."

"I wish I'd known that," said Maggie sadly.

Such misunderstandings between a husband and wife often happen when a miscarriage occurs. The father may experience many of the feelings his wife is having, but he expresses them differently, if at all.

Some men don't understand what all the fuss is about. Whenever an acquaintance of Jim's tells him that his wife has just had a miscarriage, Jim tells him to have her call me if she needs to talk. A number of them say, "It's no big thing; she's all right."

But many of those men probably feel some of the same emotions as their wives. In addition, they have unique feelings of helplessness ("my wife is suffering, and I can't do anything about it") and confusion ("what in the world is a miscarriage or an ectopic pregnancy or a blighted ovum?").

Many a father is so busy dealing with hospital personnel, taking care of the other children at home, calling relatives, and worrying about his wife's physical and emotional state that he delays showing grief until later.

Many feel something of what their wives experience, but not as intensely or for as long. Before birth, the baby is physically so much more a part of Mom than Dad that it's usually difficult for a father to relate to his child as a person until after the baby is born. While he has lost dreams, he hasn't lost a part of himself, nor has he lost his self-esteem. Most of that burden is the mother's to bear.

No matter what your husband feels, he may conceal it. Many men feel that showing they're upset will cause their wives even more pain. They think that, as caretakers of the family, they must be strong so their wives will have someone to lean on.

Even in our world of changing sex roles, a large number of men still feel it isn't masculine to cry. They may not be able to sob or to slam a door good and hard. Weeping or talking problems out with a buddy may be just too embarrassing. Worse yet, a husband who is used to being the "practical, down-to-earth type" may not even know how to identify his own feelings, which then stay locked up inside.

Some men, like Jim, plunge themselves into physical activity when they ache inside. Others, like Kathy's husband, express irrational anger. "It took me three miscarriages to understand why he always yelled at me when I started bleeding!" she says.

If you are married to a man who responds in one of these ways, you may feel misunderstood, rejected and isolated. Meanwhile, he thinks you're hanging on to your grief too long.

You may assume he doesn't feel anything for your baby, while he may be busy hiding his very real grief from himself and from you.

Conflicts can erupt. One or both of you may dig up old bones of contention that have absolutely nothing to do with the pregnancy. Perhaps you will hurl blame for the miscarriage back and forth.

It might be that, like Jim and I, you each will deal with your pain separately and shove the resulting resentment under the bed, where it can multiply like dust and old magazines.

I nurtured a number of ugly suppositions. When Jim tested the bath water the night of the miscarriage I felt positive that he blamed me for the baby's death. I also wondered if he was glad our son had died because he didn't think I was a good mother, and every criticism of my mothering seemed like new evidence against him.

Two years passed before we finally confronted our problems. But it took us another year to uncover all the "dust and magazines."

That doesn't have to happen. There are some positive things you can do.

(1) *Tell your husband exactly how you feel when you're upset,* whether you think he'll accept it or not.

(2) *Let him know what you want.* Don't expect him to read your mind. If you need a hug, ask for it. If you need to go out for a walk and think, ask him to stay with the kids. If you need him to go with you, let him know and call a babysitter.

(3) *Be affectionate.* It's hard to give affection when you're angry and depressed and physically and emotionally drained, but give it your best shot.

(4) *Talk, talk, talk!* Don't walk the long, lonely road of grief alone. Give him a chance to walk it with you.

(5) *Don't let grief smother your lives.* At first it will be your focus. After a few weeks, even if you still feel lousy, curb your outpouring of grief. A steady diet of mourning tires a man's patience. You still need to share your feelings, but try

picking a special quiet time each day for such conversations, and then concentrate with him on other things as well, if you can. If you still need to talk about it constantly, enlist the listening ear of a friend or support group. Their help should not replace his but be an addition to his input.

(6) *Don't expect him to be perfect.*

(7) *Let him express his grief in a manner different from yours.* Respect his need to run twenty miles instead of staring out the window the way you like to do. Don't accuse him of being less loving just because he loves differently.

(8) *Encourage him when he does show his emotions.* If he puts his head in your lap and cries, show him that his act of giving way to grief has made you respect him more, not less.

(9) *Don't be angry with him if he begins to enjoy life again before you do.* Everyone has his own time clock for grief.

(10) *Thank him for the things he does and says that help you.* Take nothing for granted. He needs to feel appreciated to counteract the feelings that grieving produces.

FOR HUSBANDS

When Ellen miscarried at seventeen and a half weeks, Dick was as devastated at the loss of his son as his wife was. Yet, although people were very concerned for Ellen's emotional recovery, no one ever asked how Dick was feeling.

"I was really involved in the pregnancy, and I'd built a set of dreams for the baby," says Dick. "I was hurt and angry when he died, but as a father, I was left out." A father has a great deal to grieve about when a baby dies in miscarriage. "I'll never play catch with Timothy or do any of the other things fathers do with boys," Dick says. "My expectations are gone. I held him when Ellen delivered him, but that's all I'll ever have."

Anne's husband, Joe, sees it as the loss of potential. When each of their nine babies miscarried, he mourned the fact that he would never know who that child might have been.

Especially in the case of first-time fathers, their lives had already begun to change. A baby was on the way, and life was different, even if only in their thinking and planning.

Depression and guilt feelings are common among men whose wives miscarry. Rob, a Navy pilot, was in Jacksonville, Florida, when Tricia lost their baby at home in Maine. He felt torn with feelings of failure because he wasn't there to support her when she suffered and needed him.

Fear also can attack a man when he sees his wife bleeding

or experiencing pain. Not many men know what a miscarriage is until they see it happen. When anyone is touched by death, it's natural to be afraid.

The problems a father faces in dealing with his grief are different from those his wife deals with, and what he feels is probably stronger than other people suspect. He can be feeling resentment and anger that he can't put his finger on and that he is embarrassed to admit.

It's common for a woman who miscarries to imagine that her husband will leave her because he's disappointed in her. Fear can make her clingy or cause her to distance herself in preparation for his leaving. That can confuse a man.

Since he didn't have that sense of oneness with the baby that his wife describes, a father may be scared by the intensity of his wife's sadness. It probably will last longer than he expected, causing him to wonder if she is a little unstable.

Sympathetic at first but increasingly impatient at home with his wife's lingering grief, he may find excuses to get out of the house and go someplace not so depressing. But while he's shooting pool or fishing, guilt can bubble up inside him.

It takes courage for a man to show grief immediately after a miscarriage. To express it many months later takes even more. At that point, it's tempting to forego it completely.

Finally, it's frustrating when everything he tries to do to cheer his wife up falls flat. He'd sacrifice Vikings tickets to see her smile again.

There are things a bereaved husband can do, however:

(1) *Share whatever grief you feel with your wife.* Don't be afraid that you're going to upset her further. Being able to comfort you will help her recover her self-esteem and keep her from picturing you as cold and unfeeling.

(2) *Let her grieve as much as she wants for as long as she wants.* If she suffers six months without a flicker of hope, gently suggest professional help. But if she hasn't bounced back after six weeks, don't assume she needs a psychiatrist.

(3) *Don't try to be strong for your wife.* Grieve with her. If you want to protect her, shield her from situations that might be painful, like visiting your sister who is still pregnant or her great-aunt who tends to hand out platitudes at times like these.

(4) *Try imagining what the baby would have looked like.* Grieving may be difficult for you because you feel that what you lost is nebulous. Think through how you'd have raised him, what the two of you would have done together and been to each other. It may bring you to tears, but that may be just what

you need.

(5) *Try not to feel guilty if you don't have any intense feelings about the loss.* Everyone is different.

(6) *Since you're likely to be the first one to recover, help your wife by planning a future event together.* Encourage her to get out of the house as soon as you think she's ready.

(7) *Build her self-esteem.* Find every opportunity to say positive things about her. She needs that now.

(8) *Get whatever outside support you need,* as a couple or individually. Churches, family, support groups, your closest friends — all are waiting for you to reach out.

FOR BOTH OF YOU

If you haven't gotten any other message from this chapter, I hope you've tuned in to this one: Be mutually supportive! Respect each other's feelings, differences and unique problems. You may be one couple, but you are also two individuals.

Don't demand that your routine, attitudes or relationships be the same as they were before the miscarriage. If she doesn't feel like cooking for a while, don't expect her to. Go out for a burger and tell her you love it! If the house doesn't sparkle for a time, be patient, grab a scrub brush or hire a maid.

If he uses work as therapy, meet him for lunch or pack a love note in his briefcase. If he pours out his heart to his father as well as to you, thank the Lord that he has people he can talk to who love him.

Don't blame each other for the miscarriage. If you blame yourself, it's natural to assume that the other person blames you, too. Remember, no one's at fault.

Work carefully through any ensuing sexual difficulties. The first encounter with lovemaking after a miscarriage can be a tense one. It's normal for depression, anxiety and the pressure to conceive again to decrease sexual desire in either one of you. As the bereaved mother, you may be appalled that your husband would want to make love so soon after the baby's death. *How could you want to have pleasure while I'm still mourning?* you may think. *Or, for that matter,* (here comes guilt) *how could I?*

As a bereaved father, you may fear another pregnancy (wives may share that fear). Or you may find that making love is a comforting response to your grief, and you may be upset if your wife backs away. Either of you may find lovemaking a painful reminder of how this whole nightmare started in the first place.

It's OK. I urge you to talk about your feelings. Nothing can be worked out through silence. If you're afraid of another pregnancy, use contraceptives rather than abstaining from intercourse. If you want to make love but feel guilty, talk that guilt away. You have a right to pleasure, even in the midst of pain.

Remember, too, that you can be close and loving to one another, deriving comfort and self-esteem, without actually having intercourse. Hold each other tenderly. Touch each other gently. If you decide to make love, it will be beautiful and mutual, and it will help you heal.

Need I say that turning to Christ together will be the greatest healing power of all? Jim and I can do that now, but we couldn't then. What a marvelous, healing response it would have been if we'd prayed together in our grief, gone to church side by side, squeezed each other's hands when we were hurting, and experienced the comfort of receiving communion together.

If it's possible for you to do so as a couple, reach out to God. What He provides for one of you alone He will double when you come to Him hand in hand.

Your baby was a life you helped create together. Go through his death together, too. He'd be proud to know that you are his parents.

ELEVEN

How Do the Children Feel?

The morning after my miscarriage I asked Jim how Marijean had taken the news when he told her.

"I explained that we lost the baby," he told me sheepishly "and she said, 'Don't worry, Daddy, we'll find it.'"

Once I was home, she didn't ask any questions until bedtime when she looked at me with two-and-a-half-year-old wisdom and said, "You're sad, aren't you?"

Gently I told her I was and why.

She surprised me with the intensity of her reaction. She began to cry and her chubby arms went around my neck. "But Mommy," she said, "I really wanted that baby to come here and live."

"So did I, Lovebug," I told her. "So did I."

We cried together, and then her questions came: "Why did the baby die? Is he ever coming back? Where did he go? Did it hurt when he died?"

I trod this new ground carefully, explaining that the baby wasn't strong enough to live in the world the way we did, so he was in heaven where God was taking care of him for us. When she finally drifted off to sleep, I felt close to her, as if we'd shared something precious.

In the next few months, we didn't talk much about the baby, but several times she came to me with a doll wrapped in a blanket and said, "I'm very sad. I just had this baby, but she died." I think everyone in the nursery died at least once. She pretended to cry over each one and then buried it tenderly in the dress-up box.

About six months after William's death, I ventured into our third bedroom where the family "junk" was being stored until Jim could finish the attic above our new family room. Marijean followed me in and stood gazing at the high chair and crib in the corner.

"Were those for our baby?" she asked.

"Uh-huh."

She started to cry. "I miss our baby," she said. "I really wanted him to come and play with me."

We wrapped our arms around each other and cried until all our tears were shed. She was playing happily within five minutes, but the scene stayed in my mind for days. It hurt to see *her* hurt, but it felt wonderful to know that she could feel so deeply.

VAGUE MEMORY

The subject faded from our conversation during the next few years as the business of growing from a toddler to a little girl occupied her thoughts. Then, a few months ago, it surfaced again.

We were watching a rerun of the television sitcom, *Webster,* in which Webster's adopted mother learns that she's pregnant. Webster, who had been the center of love and attention up until this point, wasn't so sure he liked the idea of a "new kid" intruding on his territory. When his mother suffered a miscarriage, he was besieged with guilt.

I was so absorbed in the episode that it took a while for me to realize that Marijean had sat through the whole show with her eyes covered.

"What's wrong?" I asked.

"I've seen this before, and I don't like it," she said. "It's too sad."

I gathered her into my arms and asked her if she remembered when that happened in our family. She searched my face, and her eyes betrayed a vague recollection rather than a definite memory.

I told her the story again, and once more she cried. There were questions this time, too, but they were different from the ones she had asked before.

"How do people die?" she asked. "Will I die? Are you going to die? Can William see us from heaven?"

We talked that night and for days afterward; I could see she was frightened by this idea of death. Fortunately, I had some wonderful children's materials on hand. We read them together and discussed the kind, loving nature of God. We talked about heaven and about grief. She wrestled with the issue until she finally seemed to come to terms with it.

It seems that her baby brother's death, and the concept of death itself, have been put to rest for now, or at least until the next stage of childhood development arrives.

PRESCHOOLERS

Marijean was typical of most young children (ages two to five) in families where miscarriage occurs. She was too young to understand what "dead" meant. It was hard for her to grasp its permanence, and she needed honesty and support to help her deal with it.

The fact that the baby went away and was never coming back meant that Mom and Dad could do that, or even that she could. The home routine had been upset by William's death, and Marijean sensed that her mommy and daddy, who were usually so in control, were anxious. Like most preschoolers, she was afraid that maybe the changes meant she wouldn't be taken care of. It was all very frightening.

Many little ones are so afraid of their new feelings that they make jokes or doggedly continue their normal play as a distraction. Some regress into such things as bedwetting, thumbsucking, tantrums or reattachment to a favorite object.

Others try to make sense out of what's going on by acting out stories where stuffed animals die and go to make-believe heavens or miraculously come back to life. Still others talk about death incessantly, dream about it, or draw pictures that reflect their ideas about death.

It isn't unusual for new fears to creep into their lives. Their first illness after the baby's death might be particularly disturbing to them. They also may feel angry toward the baby, certain that he or she could come back and play if he really wanted to.

OLDER CHILDREN

Children who are six years old or older at the time of the miscarriage, or when they bring up the subject, usually can accept the finality of death but often relate it to themselves. Anne's daughter was seven when Anne had a miscarriage at home. Suddenly her daughter began to ask questions. When Anne talked of the nine babies she'd lost, her daughter was considerably disturbed. "I'm here," she said to her mother, "but I might not have been."

Until they're about nine, children may dwell on the idea of spirits and angels, heaven and hell. They seem to view death as a person, place or thing, or some sort of ghost. To them, a dark room and death are the same; they're afraid of the unknown and the emptiness they associate with it. It isn't until they're about ten that they start to form realistic concepts.

Their behavior may change too as they confront death. They may become more withdrawn or more aggressive. They may avoid the subject of death at first, making blithe comments or shouting with abandon to relieve tension. They're protecting themselves from something they find frightening. They may need to ponder the event before talking about it to give themselves time to absorb its impact.

In kids of this age, feelings may show up days after the fact and may occur over something unrelated to the death. Usually the emotions burst and then vanish — for a while.

A young person might express how left out he feels with everyone so concerned about Mom and the baby. He may hint that if you're upset over a lost child, you must not be satisfied with the one you have. Some "mourn at a distance,"[1] showing tremendous empathy for characters in a book or deeply mourning a broken or lost possession.

Another child might deal with death by telling other people what happened. Being so anxious to spread the news might seem inappropriate to you, but it's a child's natural way of letting out built-up tension and being part of what's going on.

ADOLESCENTS

Adolescents can grasp the idea of death with all its by-products, and they may react in much the same way as their parents do, with anger, guilt and sadness. The event may have a personal significance to them, and fear of *their* death may crop up. Newly blessed with the ability to think abstractly, they may focus on why it happened and whose fault it was and become angry in the process. Teens who were embarrassed by their "older" mother's pregnancy may now feel guilty about those thoughts. Adolescent girls who are just beginning to identify with motherhood may experience a set of fears that are new to them.

Children of any age respond deeply to the feelings of the people they love, and they are affected by the death of an unborn brother or sister, whether they show it or not. It can be a difficult experience for them. Being in a safe, accepting environment makes it easier for them to express their concerns and pass through the trauma and the grieving process into richer lives.[2]

HELPING YOUR CHILD UNDERSTAND

The following do's and don'ts can guide you as you attempt to help your child understand and accept your miscarriage.

DO:

(1) *Raise the issue if the child doesn't.* Find opportunities to bring it up in your daily routine, probing for fears the child may have that he (or she) caused the baby's death by his jealousy, or that, because you're so upset, you must love the baby more than you love him.

(2) *Tell adults who are important in the child's life, such as teachers and babysitters, what happened and how you're handling it.*

(3) *Let the child speak openly and don't judge or criticize anything he says.* He shouldn't experience any guilt or shame because of his feelings.

(4) *Reassure him that most people live long lives and that the rest of the family probably will also.*

(5) *Talk together about the memories you have of the pregnancy.* Use the baby's name. It will make the loss seem more real to your child, and it will help him be a part of a constructive family resolution. After all, it is the *family's* crisis.

(6) *If your child flounders in grieving for a baby he's never seen, help him find a way to say goodbye.* Perhaps plan an informal family memorial service or say a prayer together. You might want to give something you had for the baby to your child. Marijean's Cabbage Patch doll wears a pair of William's booties to this day.

(7) *If your child wants to talk but you're too upset, promise that you will talk soon. Then keep your promise.*

(8) *Express your emotions and explain them to your child.* Children are so sensitive to parental moods, and if your child doesn't understand those moods, he may experience fears which can last for a very long time. Being transparent with him allows you to model appropriate grieving responses that he will draw on and reproduce in his own future crises.

(9) *Answer his questions honestly and directly.* When he asks you something and you don't know the answer, admit it. The more openly you communicate, the less room you leave for unfounded fears.

(10) *Let your child comfort you, and show him how much you appreciate his efforts.* The small gesture of tucking a treasured teddy bear into bed beside you or sharing a gooey graham cracker will make a child feel he's helping, and it *will* make you feel better. You can't help but value what you *do* have at a time like this. Older children can do practical things to help that will make them feel important. Teens often are more thoughtful, concerned and communicative than we give them credit for, so give them a chance to show it when you need it most.

(11) *Tell your child the facts before he overhears conversations that can be misconstrued.* After a fourth miscarriage, the Johnsons' son Stephen heard a friend say to his father, "I think it's time for you to stop trying. What's going to happen to you and those boys if Kathy dies one of these times?" Stephen began following his mother, terrified to let her out of his sight. It took some time for them to relieve his fear.

(12) *Lavish love on your child.* He desperately needs to know that you love *him*, too.

(13) *Make time for your child in spite of your grief.* You may feel that dealing with him is more than you can handle when your grief seems unbearable, but it will be worth it. Guiding Marijean through the experience lifted my self-esteem and made me realize that I really was a good mother.

(14) *Tell an older child how to explain the loss to other people.* It can be awkward for him, and he needs your guidance.

(15) *Watch for behavior changes.* Handle them with understanding rather than punishment.

DON'T:

(1) *Don't become overprotective — or overpermissive.*

(2) *Don't cut your child's feelings short by saying, "Be brave," or "Don't cry."* Especially don't say this to a boy! At the same

time, don't try to make a child act out something he doesn't feel.

(3) *Don't give inappropriate explanations.* Some examples would be:

- "We lost the baby." Some children have developed fears of closets where the lost baby might be lurking.
- "The baby went to sleep." This can result in children having problems with sleeping.
- "The baby went away." Your child may fear his own separation from you.
- "The baby *got sick* and died." The child may become frightened that if he gets sick, or if you do, death may result.
- "God needed a little angel in heaven," or "God wanted the baby to come and live with Him." To little ears, these explanations make God sound like an ogre who may swoop down unexpectedly and take him or either of his parents to be an angel, too.

Instead of the above, tell your child, "The baby died." That's what the child needs to know.

(4) *Don't ship your child off to a friend's or relative's house for a long stay.* If you need to be alone to grieve, ask someone to take the child for brief periods only. He needs your reassuring presence in order to feel he is a part of what the family is going through.

An unborn baby's death can be a time to begin educating a child about death. That part of being a parent isn't much fun, but it's one of the most important parts.

There are many excellent books on the market for children of all ages that you and your kids can read together. For a list of some suggestions, see Appendix V at the end of this book. Information, shared by loving parents, is vital.

Handled properly, children can learn to grasp the finality of death and can understand their right to grieve. They can learn how to mourn, and they can develop healthy patterns for grieving that they'll carry with them and that will help them when they face losses in the future. When they see you turn to the Lord for comfort, they will see God as a compassionate father who takes care of those who die *and* of those who are left behind. Helping your children realize that our Lord hurts when we hurt can bring them closer to Him.

What finer gift can we give our children?

TWELVE

Can I Depend on My Medical Support Group?

The morning after my D & C, Dr. Breeden hurried into my hospital room, his eyes full of sympathy and his hands ready to give my arms a loving squeeze.

"I really didn't think this was going to happen," he said. "If I'd known, I'd have been here, even though I wasn't on call."

With the exception of one hurried office nurse and the "sergeant" in the emergency room two months before, all my contacts with medical personnel were reassuring and affirming. I'll never forget the genuine concern on Dr. Myers's face as he searched for the baby's heartbeat. Or the nurse who asked the next morning if my husband was sympathetic to the miscarriage, and who made sure I was going to get plenty of hugs at home.

"They all treated us with respect," Jim recalls now. "Nobody tried to hurry us through any decision or tried to make it for us. I really appreciated that."

Others report similar experiences. Roseanna feels that she was able to accept her miscarriage at four weeks more easily because her doctor called her at home the week afterward to reassure her.

When Ellen miscarried at seventeen and a half weeks, their

doctor allowed her and Dick and their ten-year-old daughter to hold their baby boy for as long as they liked.

I've learned, however, that not every couple has an understanding group of doctors and nurses to validate their loss and comfort them in their confusion and grief.

DISTRESSING EXPERIENCES

Six years after her seventeen-week miscarriage, Ann's soft Southern voice still rose in anger when we talked about it long-distance.

"I started spotting five or six weeks before the actual miscarriage, and I was told by my doctor to stay in bed, which I did. I was never told what to expect or what would happen, so every time I had any symptom I called the doctor, and he made me feel like a pest. I went in to see him seven or eight times during this period and was told every time that everything was fine. I knew when I'd conceived and told him so. But he said I was not as far along as I thought I was. 'Well,' he said, 'that would mean the baby isn't growing.' — which was precisely my point all along! But he never took me seriously.

"Finally, at seventeen weeks, I started having what felt like labor pains. I called the doctor and he told me to go straight to the hospital, a seventy-mile trip. My water broke en route, so since my doctor's office was on the way, we stopped there first. They said again to go straight to the hospital.

"And don't you know," she said, her voice shaking, "the first thing he said to me when he walked in was, 'If you had called first, you could have saved yourself the emergency room fee'! Then he examined me, all the while making wisecracks. He told me I had had a miscarriage, gave orders for blood and for reserving the operating room — and left. It was the nurse who explained that he couldn't stop the bleeding, and they were going to do an emergency D & C."

Eight years after her miscarriage, Robin, too, became distressed and angry when we discussed her obstetrician.

"I became pregnant while using a Dalkon Shield IUD, and when I went to the doctor, I disliked him immediately. He was so impersonal and insensitive. He took the position that since I was using a contraceptive, I didn't want a baby anyway, so the outcome wouldn't make much difference to me! To him it meant nothing. It never occurred to him that it was part of Jerry and me, that it was going to be our baby.

"He was unable to remove the IUD because of its position,

and he warned me about the possibility of a miscarriage, but he didn't mention my chances of developing a dangerous infection — which is what happened. I had to learn from the *Donahue Show* months later that 50 percent of the women who develop that kind of infection *die!*

"I was in a lot of pain and my fever was 103° when we finally called him, just one day before I was five months pregnant. He met us at the hospital, strode in, examined me, and said, 'You are aborting.' That was it!

"He seemed very annoyed by my questions, especially when I asked, 'Is there any chance the baby could live?'

"He sort of snorted and said, 'No, absolutely none.'

"I distrusted him so much by then that I insisted Jerry be allowed to be in the next room while I delivered the baby. And even then, as I was lying there crying, the doctor brought in three student nurses. He said, 'Here we have a thirty-one-year-old . . .'

"I just couldn't take that. I said, 'Excuse me. My name is Mrs. Wolf, and I am not a cow. I will not have these students in here while I'm delivering my BABY!' Only then did he begin to treat me with a little bit of respect."

The mothers' list of complaints goes on.

Kathy is jarred by the unfeeling use of medical language: *termination, fetal wastage, habitual aborter,* etc. "They call my loss a 'spontaneous abortion,' and my baby the 'products of conception.' They don't understand the dreams I have already invested in this baby."

When Anne and her husband, Joe, decided to continue trying to have another baby after a genetic translocation was discovered, their doctors hounded them about the possibility of having a baby with Down's syndrome and endlessly criticized their decision.

Fortunately, with the awareness that has come from support groups and hospital programs, these kinds of scenes are changing. But there is still enough misunderstanding and emotional hurt going on in doctors' offices and emergency and operating rooms to warrant some discussion.

SOME HELPFUL ANSWERS

In my talks with women who have suffered miscarriages and ectopic pregnancies, and with the men who have suffered beside those women, I've heard several questions asked over and over that need answers. Assisted by support people all over the country, I've found some answers that I think might be helpful.

Why don't doctors prepare a woman for the possibility of a miscarriage?

Often they do, but in her excitement she chooses not to hear it. It's something that happens to the proverbial "other people."

Some doctors don't bring up the subject, thinking, "Why worry a patient with something that has an 80 percent chance of not happening?"[1]

It's a thought worth pondering: Would it have made any difference if someone had warned you?

Why are some doctors surprised when you're upset over a miscarriage?

Some doctors see miscarriage as a natural screening process and don't recognize that the parents consider the loss a *baby.* Looking at things from a clinical standpoint, the doctor may view the miscarriage as a minor medical event and forget that it is a devastating personal one to the parents.

Why does my doctor treat my ectopic pregnancy as just "major surgery"?

In many cases, ectopic pregnancy is still a cause of maternal death, due to internal hemorrhage. A doctor who has successfully brought a patient through surgery for an ectopic may be so relieved that she's alive that he may put aside the fact that the mother has lost her child and her chances of having a successful pregnancy in the future have been reduced. "It's a real revelation to some doctors to discover patients who think of an ectopic pregnancy as the loss of a baby," says Dr. Rochelle Friedman, co-author of *Surviving Pregnancy Loss.*[2]

Why do some doctors immediately conclude that you have psychological problems if you've had three or more miscarriages?

Because many of them were trained to think that!

In the past, and unfortunately sometimes even now, doctors think of women who are "habitual aborters" as neurotic personality types and they attribute to emotional factors any problem for which they are unable to identify a specific medical cause. Again, times are changing and, in all fairness, we must recognize that doctors are becoming more aware that psychological factors are the result of repeated miscarriages rather than the cause.

Why don't some doctors have any feelings when it comes

to a miscarriage or an ectopic pregnancy?

My guess is that they do care. An excerpt from Nancy Berezin's book, *After a Loss in Pregnancy,* convinced me of that: "There is no obstetrician who has not strained through a stethoscope to catch only the sickening silence of an absent fetal heartbeat. Common sense and compassion tell him that his facial expression must not betray his anxiety. He tells himself that *surely the heartbeat is somewhere . . . it's just hiding . . . I must not scare the patient."[3]*

Traditionally, medical professionals haven't been trained to deal with patients' grief over their loss. They are too busy, and rightly so, learning to save lives. The obstetrician is the least likely of the medical specialists to have spent any time learning to help patients cope with death. It's his (or her) job to bring *life* into the world, squalling and squirming amid the joyous shouts of parents.

The failure of a pregnancy may even spell personal failure to the doctor. That callous, unfeeling face you see may really be a mask that covers his own anguish. His clinical detachment may be his way of hiding the nagging feeling that he has let you down. When a doctor feels guilty and inadequate, even when there is no basis for that feeling, it may be easier just to leave and let the nurse explain everything.

That coldness may also be a defense. Perhaps he's afraid of intensifying your grief by saying something touching like, "I'm sorry." Maybe he's nervous that you will hurl accusations at him, so he wants to get out of your room *fast.* Maybe he has been so inured by the you-can't-get-involved-with-every-patient philosophy that he's afraid seeing you upset will overwhelm him, too.

WHAT WE CAN DO

"M.D." doesn't stand for Medical Divine. Doctors are people, too, and they make mistakes. As Christians, we can forgive them when those mistakes hurt our feelings. As responsible adult patients, we can help them rectify their errors. Here's how:

(1) *Don't pretend to feel courage and acceptance when you are with your doctor if that isn't what you feel.* Many of us don't realize that while we're yearning for a hug or a sympathetic word, we're also attempting to appear brave and controlled. We may look as stiff-necked as the expressionless doctor does.

(2) *Make sure you don't project your own reactions onto your*

doctor. Was he abrupt with you, or were you angry with yourself? Anger is a natural part of grief, and the doctor is often the safest person to get mad at because you don't have to live with him every day.[4] But did he really instill false hope in you early in the pregnancy, or were you so anxious for it to go full term that you didn't listen carefully? I'm not suggesting that the doctor is never ill-tempered or bad-mannered, but it's certainly worth a close look.

(3) *Stand up for yourself by making your wants and needs clear.* If you want answers to questions, insist on them. If you want reassurance that you'll be able to have more children, ask for it. If you want diagnostic tests, insist on them.

After two miscarriages Pat had had enough. Instead of submitting to her doctor's "rule" that she have four miscarriages before he ran tests, she wrote letters, did research, made phone calls — and got the tests she wanted. Because of those tests, a treatable problem was found, and her next pregnancy produced a healthy, yellow-haired cherub.

(4) *If you don't get the satisfaction you need, change doctors.*

Lynda Madaras and Jane Patterson, both M.D.s and the authors of *Womancare*, say that most of us spend more time choosing a new dress than we do choosing a doctor. They suggest that you collect names of physicians to interview for the job of being your obstetrican. A list of obstetricians and gynecologists is available at most hospitals. Other women are also reliable references.

Evaluate the doctors' credentials, being sure they are board certified and members of the American College of Gynecologists and Obstetricians. Check out their personal styles to find one you feel comfortable with. Find out who is willing to answer questions and who can do so with a clear explanation,[5] and without making you feel that you're being difficult or are being talked down to. Seek out someone who doesn't believe in psychogenic causes for habitual abortion or who shares your beliefs about the value of life in the womb. If you have a specific problem, such as infertility or a history of repeated miscarriages, locate a specialist who is sensitive and skilled in treating that problem.

SUPPORT GROUPS

Fortunately, many hospitals are now developing programs designed specifically to help the medical personnel who serve families suffering a pregnancy loss. Through training programs, seminars, and literature, medical people are learning that even a single miscarriage can leave emotional scars that may last a lifetime,[6] and that while the required medical treatment may be routine, the giving of emotional support is highly specialized.

A.M.E.N.D., which stands for Aiding a Mother and Father Experiencing Neonatal Death, is a forerunner in this movement to sensitize and inform medical personnel. Based in St. Louis, Missouri, A.M.E.N.D. has chapters across the country that work with hospitals and help parents who suffer any kind of pregnancy loss. Its concern is that hospital personnel provide grieving parents with every possible option that will aid them in the mourning process, including such things as where the mother stays while she is in the hospital and deciding what is to be done with the baby's body.

Many individual support groups also have begun to develop programs to educate local hospital personnel.

Another organization, Resolve Through Sharing, affiliated with the LaCrosse Lutheran Hospital/Gundersen Clinic, Ltd., in LaCrosse, Wisconsin, offers among its many services a three-day course for medical professionals. It teaches them the skills they need to respond helpfully to families who lose a baby through miscarriage, stillbirth or newborn death. Sara Wheeler and Rana Limbo, both registered nurses with master's degrees, have trained personnel in such major cities as San Diego, Phoenix, Chicago and Philadelphia. There are now thirteen Resolve Through Sharing hospitals nationwide.

Even small-scale support groups, such as Kinder-Mourn in Charlotte, North Carolina, offer in-service training for professionals. Each one helps medical people study the grieving process and develop the skills they need to help parents through the tragedy of losing a baby.

Many of these programs are spearheaded by active Christians who see a need for the Lord's hand in the education of doctors, nurses and hospital staff.

Sister Jane Marie Lamb of St. John's Hospital in Springfield, Illinois, is one of these.

"For all too long, little has been done," she wrote me, "and I feel that if the churches do not respond, they have neglected a most important area." With the help of Sister Jane Marie, St. John's began allowing parents who wanted to bury their babies to do so as a form of actualizing their loss. The hospitals that are under her supervision provide keepsakes, offer to baptize babies, and provide the emotional support grieving parents need.

The day is over when a mother must automatically accept

the fact that her doctor may treat her coldly or that her nurses will fail to understand what she's experiencing when she suffers a miscarriage. But there is still much to be done to educate medical personnel everywhere. This ministry waits for Christians, as we'll see in a future chapter.

For now, know that there *are* doctors who truly want to give their patients good emotional care as well as adequate physical treatment. If yours is one, thank him. If he isn't, forgive him, and find one who can give you the Christian love you need and deserve.

THIRTEEN

Where Are My Family and Friends When I Need Them?

After my miscarriage our family and friends showered us with sympathy. I was touched by their phone calls, notes and flowers. Everyone I called (and I'm sure I called *everyone!*) willingly listened as I poured out our story. Several friends even dropped by that weekend to help with meals and with Marijean's care.

But as the days went by, some people began suggesting that I should be "over it" by now. When was I going to pull myself together? Wasn't it time to get on with my life?

Others acted as if nothing had happened. They never mentioned our loss or asked how I was feeling.

They were part of the reason I buried my pain and concentrated on finding intellectual answers without ever resolving my grief. With so many people shaking their heads and wondering about the state of my mental health, it seemed irrational to continue feeling sad and to go on talking about my pain. I let their opinions about how I should feel determine how I handled my grief.

More than a year later when I could no longer hide my grief, I became deeply depressed. However, I did know and act on these two facts:

(1) *The right people can help you tremendously in the grieving process.*
(2) *The wrong people can hurt you immeasurably if you allow them to undermine your grief.*

SOMEONE TO LISTEN

When I began grieving again, I didn't share my grief with everyone. I'm sure most people were aware that something was amiss when I dropped ten pounds and cried at the slightest provocation, but only a few special people were privy to my agony.

My friend Barb was one. She stood in her kitchen for hours, wiping down the counter top in soothing strokes while I sat on a stool, drinking herb tea and churning out all my feelings.

She listened. She nodded. She gave an occasional murmur of understanding. And when she thought I was ready, she gave me things to think about.

She invited Marijean and me to share the weekend with her and her family when Jim went out of town. She insisted I spend the day at her house one morning when I simply couldn't go to work.

She knew when to lift my spirits with a joke. She knew when to lift my self-esteem by sharing some of her own problems. She knew when to leave me a note at school, and when to put a present on my pillow, and when to leave me alone. She was one of God's gifts.

Sam, our minister, was another. He sat at his desk, rocking back and forth in his swivel chair, while I talked in what seemed like endless circles. He never judged. He never quoted Scripture. He just listened to me and loved me.

He called on the phone to see how I was doing. When he thought I was ready, he began to give me things to do in the church, jobs that tapped my true flair for ministry. Most of all, he prayed with me and for me.

Richard, one of my co-workers at the high school, was another caring friend. I didn't know Richard well, but the Lord planted him in my life and he sensed my need to grieve and to have a friend stand by me while I mourned.

Every morning before school began, he brought a cup of home-brewed tea to my classroom. He let me cry without saying a word. He brought me books and poems that calmed my spirit. He asked me the right questions, but he never pushed me to answer them. He always seemed to be there at the moments when I wanted to give it all up.

My sister-in-law, Penny, was one more such friend. She hugged me and forced me to reach inside myself for answers when I was tempted to blame my feelings on hormones and simply wait for the cloud to pass. She gave me a safe place to scream out my anger and a lap to put my head in when I needed to sob. Most important of all, she cried with me because she loved William Bradley, too.

I never worried that any of those people were going to get tired of me and my sorrows. I knew I needed their help, and I knew they loved me enough to give it.

Christine Palinski, co-author of *Coping With a Miscarriage*, says the power of sharing feelings during times of crisis mustn't be underestimated. Coping with pain and death is so much easier in an open, supportive environment.[1]

Sometimes it takes a friend or a loved one to give you permission to grieve. Talking about your baby's death, over and over, helps you cope with the situation and somehow make it an acceptable part of your experience. In fact, it may be the only time for a while when you actually feel like a real person. "The grief that does not speak," wrote Shakespeare, "whispers the o'erfraught heart and bids it break."[2]

Probably most important of all, friends in your life can give you the love you need to help you rediscover your value as a person when you have become lost in the folds of depression. Christian friends can help you see yourself from God's point of view again.

"God has not promised us a life free of the pain of crisis," writes Juanita Ryan in her book, *Standing By*, "but He has given us each other to minister His love and presence during these times."[3]

RIGHT TO GRIEVE

Studies have shown that the length and intensity of your recovery is both positively and negatively affected by the attitudes of those around you.[4] Others can inflict as much guilt and doubt as they can bestow comfort.

I avoided the people who I knew wouldn't understand. If I had to be around them, I finished our business as quickly as possible. When they said, "What are you so tense about?" or, "What do you have to be depressed over?" I said, "Evidently quite a bit, or I wouldn't feel this way." And I forgave them. They hadn't brushed shoulders with sorrow in the way that I had yet, so how could they understand?

When people make you feel that you shouldn't mourn so, you may find yourself defending your right to grieve. When you're still grieving after six weeks, or when you feel great and then experience a setback around the time of the baby's due date, some people may be baffled. These people usually can't grasp the psychological impact of a miscarriage.

Others — the ones who have trouble dealing with their own sorrow and pain — may realize you're hurting but will try to cheer you up instead of letting you work through it. They haven't come to terms with the idea of death yet, so they'd rather not face it with you. They'd rather hear that you've bounced back. It hurts when other people view your loss as something that can be fixed up right away with a smile and an ice cream sundae.

There are also the unfortunate few Christians who will tell you that if you'd had more faith, the baby would have lived; that if you really trusted in the Lord, you could accept the loss as God's will and go on without a tear; that you should fight your sadness, because depression is Satan's attack.[5] It's hard in your doubt-ridden state not to let these people get you down.

Then there are those who minimize your loss with "practical" ideas. "You already have children at home," they tell you, "so be thankful for what you have. Would you have wanted a deformed or retarded child? Wouldn't it have been much worse to have carried the baby to term and had it die then? It seems to me it was meant to be. And besides, you're young, you have your health, you can always have other children — and do it soon, because your child needs a brother or sister." Or they say, "You're having such a hard time that you really shouldn't have any more children; it's not good for you. But cheer up. Millions of other women have been through it, and they got over it."

"I hated it when people said, 'It was a good thing. Your kids would have been too close together'!" Paula told me.

"I hated it when people said, 'It was a boy, and God knew you wanted a girl,'" says Kathy. "As if He didn't know before I conceived that I wanted a girl!"

"My in-laws had the nerve to suggest that it was just as well, because we couldn't afford another baby anyway!" Linda said.

"Our baby weighed eleven ounces and was almost nine inches long," says Ellen. "But people still implied that he wasn't a baby. Yet when the Frustaci's had their seven babies at once, they were the same size, and no one criticized her when she mourned the one that was stillborn."

Those are all comments that may help you in the future, but they do you no good when you're in pain. They only make you feel angry and guilty, because intellectually you *know* one thing, but emotionally you *feel* something else.

Perhaps the people who hurt you the most are the ones you thought would be there for you but who seem to ignore the whole thing. Their silence doesn't mean they don't care. They simply may be so afraid of saying the wrong thing that they say nothing.

Or perhaps they, too, are in the process of bearing children and are afraid to confront the possibility of pregnancy loss. By avoiding you, they avoid the subject.

Or perhaps someone they once tried to comfort lashed out in anger, so they are protecting themselves from the possibility of another such onslaught.

While your parents can be a source of comfort to you when your baby dies, as both my mother and Jim's parents were, they can be a source of confusion, too.

"I remember my mother coming and staying with me," Suzanne recalls. "She went around washing windows because she didn't know what to say, and my mother can always find something comforting to say."

That may be because your folks are dealing with their own grief. They've lost a grandchild they were looking forward to having, and now they realize they've also lost the ability to make you feel better instantly as they did when you were a child. It's hard for them to watch you suffer from the death of your baby, and they may make the mistake of saying things to try to make you feel better. They may even try to "mother" you with statements like, "I told you that you weren't eating right."

You *want* someone to say, "You have a right to feel awful." You *want* someone to say, "You are strong. You can get through this." Yet your mother may say, "It's all right. You can have another baby," and with her trite platitudes make you feel like a helpless child who can't keep the situation in perspective.

FINDING SUPPORT

What can you do? You need people, yet when you try to reach out, some of them bite your hand.

First, *claim your right to feel the way you feel.* Don't be afraid to disagree with their comments, but don't attack the people who anger you. Try saying, "I don't agree with you. It means a whole lot more than that to us."

Second, *eliminate some of the misunderstanding by the way you announce the news of your loss.* Dick found that if he said, "We lost a son," rather than, "My wife had a miscarriage," people took the event much more seriously.

Third, *forgive those folks who seem to have forgotten you.* Seeing you in pain is probably painful for them, and most likely they don't know what to do. Be like Job and forgive those who blow their attempt to be helpful, and follow Peter's advice about not holding a grudge (1 Peter 2:23). As Joy and Marvin Johnson point out in the Centering Corporation's booklet, *Miscarriage,* at least when they offer the "awkward gifts given in good faith," they're trying to help.[6]

Fourth, *build a support network of people who understand you and know how to help.*

The most comforting people are those who have faced and accepted their own response to death. These are usually mature Christians and people who have suffered a loss themselves. They won't be afraid to hear about your doubts, fears and snarls of anger. They won't automatically respond with portions of Scripture. They'll know you have to work through your grief.

You also can draw support from other women who have had miscarriages. The victims of pregnancy loss who talked with me assured me that the pain does end and that there can be other babies, but that it's OK to feel horrible right now. They were the ones who would talk all day on that one subject, who would listen to all the details, maybe even more than once. They were the ones who showed me I wasn't a failure.

That kind of understanding is the foundation for parent support groups, a subject we'll look at in depth in the next chapter. If you don't know anyone who has suffered a loss in pregnancy, a support group may be for you.

There, new friendships can spring from shared grief. In fact, a new friendship can occur when anyone you weren't previously close to says the right words or does the right things when you're in emotional turmoil.

Any person you turn to should be someone who accepts your emotions, confirms the reality and the significance of what you've lost and helps you see your way to the future.[7] He or she should be like our Lord Jesus: available, humble, empathetic and full of vision.[8]

Where do you find these people? Hopefully in the church.

YOUR CHURCH FAMILY

Caring for others in a crisis should be a community affair, says Juanita Ryan, and that's where the church can and should volunteer.[9] Christians know it's OK to lean on other people. Christians are a people full of hope, yet they possess compassion for the person caught in a hopeless moment. Christians may bungle their attempts at comfort just as badly as anyone else, but they have enough love to make up for what they lack in finesse.

If you belong to a church family, turn to it. If the Spirit is there, arms will open to you. People will know what to do.

If you don't have a church home, now would be a good time to find your place in the Christian community. Don't feel that churches will turn you away because you waited for tragedy to strike before darkening their door. Your membership in the church family can start with sorrow and grow from there.

When you find such people, help them help you.

(1) *Let people know what you need.* If you want to be hugged or listened to or allowed to cry in someone's arms, say so. Tell them you need to hear that you're still wonderful, or let them know that you'd love to go to lunch or that you'd like a few hours alone without your two-year-old. Tell them you're too depressed to cook tonight and that you'd appreciate a pot of their great vegetable soup. How many times have you said to someone in the midst of a crisis, "If there's anything I can do, let me know"? People mean it.

(2) *If you want to talk about the miscarriage and no one brings it up, lead into it yourself.* Your friends may be unsure how to get you talking. Remember that if *you* act as if nothing happened, so will they.

You may find that you repeat yourself, ask the same questions over and over or become angry with the person who is trying to show she cares about you. That's OK. It's all part of the grieving process.

(3) *Educate your friends.* If they've never lost a baby, they may not know that you want your baby referred to as "the baby" or "Kevin" or "Jennifer" rather than "it." They may not realize that to you it wasn't "just a miscarriage" — it was the death of your child.

(4) *If you have a memorial service, you may want to include your friends.* One of the reasons funerals were created was to give family and friends a socially acceptable way of expressing concern for a bereaved person.

(5) *Be especially open with your friends who are pregnant.* Find out if your experience frightens them. Reassure them that they have a better chance of carrying their baby to term than of losing it through miscarriage. If you'd rather not see them

until you've gotten past your anger, tell them. If you want them around to remind you that pregnancies are often healthy, let them know.

(6) *Make a list of the loving, supportive things people do for you.* According to the Johnsons, it can be a positive reminder for the times when you need good memories.

(7) *Thank those who stand by you.* None of us helps another just to receive a reward, but it's sure nice to hear their gratitude expressed.

As you help your friends and family help you in your sorrow, you'll be giving them a lesson in grieving. Everyone faces grief sometime, and allowing them to share your sorrow and watch you pull through it and grow into a better, stronger person will be an inspiration to them that they may need in the future. That inspiration alone may make your baby's short life worthwhile.

FOURTEEN

Support — From *Strangers?*

As I left Sacramento and headed back to Dayton, my mind was teeming with ideas. I was excited, fulfilled and up to my ear lobes in new information.

The only unhappy thought that crept into my mind was, *Why? Why wasn't a support group around for us when we lost our baby?*

As part of my research for this book, I spent four hours with members of the Sacramento, California, Sharing Parents miscarriage support group, one of eighty chapters of the national organization, SHARE (Source of Help in Airing and Resolving Experiences). Six mothers, a father, and a ten-year-old daughter gave up their day to share their experiences with me and let me see firsthand what a childbirth-loss support group is like.

I went there for information, but I came away with a great deal more. I felt touched by other people's private, secret, inside lives. I was reassured that everything I felt and everything I was writing about was normal and healthy — even productive. Probably most important of all, I was unexpectedly surrounded with Christian love.

SOCIAL/MEDICAL SUPPORT GROUPS

What a blessing it would have been if Jim and I could have had that fellowship when William Bradley died. What we needed and what many couples need who have suffered a miscarriage is the very thing a mutual help support group provides.

"The single most important need of the bereaved," wrote Sister Jane Marie Lamb, "is to have a social network of support — people we can share our pain with over and over."[1]

Fortunately, such social networks designed specifically for parents who have lost babies in miscarriage, stillbirth and newborn death, are multiplying across the United States. Some groups are chapters of national programs. Others are springing up independently out of the needs of individual communities. But all have the same reason for being.

According to one of its brochures, the purpose of the Sharing Parents support group is "to provide an atmosphere where grieving parents with similar experiences can come together and share their feelings about their loss. It is also a place where parents express the love they had for their baby . . . where they can give and receive emotional support by sharing common experiences and learn about the natural grief process, while working through and resolving their loss. Parents learn that the intensity and longevity of their feelings are normal, and that their problems and anxieties are shared by other bereaved parents."[2]

If two weeks pass after the day of your loss and friends and family are no longer calling as often as they did at first but you're still struggling with the pain and sadness, it might be a good idea to take out the phone book and search through the yellow pages for support groups that may be affiliated with local hospitals. Or search the white pages for the names of national organizations such as SHARE, Resolve Through Sharing, The Compassionate Friends, P.E.P.D. (Parents Experiencing Perinatal Death) or A.M.E.N.D. Professionals or lay counselors will tell you what services they offer, when their groups meet and how you can reach someone who will talk with you immediately, while you're hurting.

If you can't find a group in your area, write to: National Perinatal Bereavement Coalition, St. Mary's Health Center, 6420 Clayton Road, St. Louis, MO 63117, and ask for the group located nearest you.

NOT A THERAPY GROUP

Perhaps the idea of a "therapy" group doesn't appeal to you.

It may carry connotations of 1970s encounter groups or smack of some morbid or impersonal team of psychiatrists delving into people's private worlds. If you're already frightened by the intensity of your emotions, you might be put off by the still-present social stigma of psychotherapy. Or you may be convinced that reaching out for help, especially from strangers, is a sign of weakness.

You'll be pleasantly surprised to hear the facts on each of these topics.

First, a support group is not a therapy group. It simply provides what it says — support — through the interaction of group members. No records are kept, no analyzing is done. There is listening. There is understanding of grief. There is sharing of pain. There are no time limits, no fees, no confrontation, no pressure. Each person is merely helped to make it through each day until he or she can begin to "live" again.[3]

Second, there is nothing morbid about such gatherings. As The Compassionate Friends organization states, "We acknowledge the pain that is a part of loving. We have loved, therefore, we grieve. We are willing to share someone's sorrow."[4]

Third, meetings often center around a topic presented to the group by a professional. An opportunity for questions and discussion follows. Usually after a break and refreshments, the group splits into small groups for another brief session when parents can air their personal feelings and the problems they face. Everyone participates, whether she or he just listens, offers insight to the others, or reaches out for help.

BENEFITS

Fourth, the list of benefits you can receive from belonging to a support group is long:

(1) *You'll discover that the feelings you experience are normal.* No one will think you are bizarre or that you are over-reacting to a trivial loss. You will never become a burden to the group members. One group facilitator, from Kinder-Mourn in Charlotte, North Carolina, says, "To me, one of the best things that happens [in a support group] is that [participants] start to accept their craziness as normal, and it begins to take some of the pressure off."[5]

(2) *You'll feel close to others* at a time when you may have been feeling very much alone.

(3) *You'll be able to ventilate all your emotions* without embarrassment, without fear of being judged or criticized, and

without having your loss minimized by someone who sup-
posedly "lost more" than you did. There is no comparison
of grief. Everyone's sorrow is considered valid.

(4) *You'll explore possible solutions to the problems* that arise
during your recovery. It is a matter of, as one mother called
it, "artfully crafting one another's broken hearts and dreams
into forms of hope."[6]

(5) *You'll receive encouragement whenever you need it,* which
will probably be often at first.

(6) *You'll have a place to cry* where no one will try to stop you.

(7) *You'll have a neutral context in which you and your spouse
can meet to understand better the differences in your grief.*
Fathers are almost always welcome to attend.

(8) *You may stay with the group as long as you like.* You may
want to receive help with a subsequent pregnancy or even
in adjusting to the arrival of your next baby.

(9) *You may gain access to a lending library.* Many groups also
provide an initial grief packet to parents before they leave
the hospital. Resolve Through Sharing, of LaCrosse, Wisconsin,
recently sent me their packet to help me in writing this
book. If I'd had something like that when our baby died,
I'd have been spared some unnecessary heartache.

(10) As you begin to resolve your grief, *you'll be able to help
new members of the group whose hurts are fresh.* Sharing
how you coped, and boosting someone else's spirit, will do
wonders for your self-esteem.

(11) If you're so inclined, *you may even find opportunities through
the support group to educate the community* on the subject
of pregnancy loss.

SPECIAL PROGRAMS

Many groups provide special programs. Kinder-Mourn holds
a Holiday Memorial Service before Christmas as a time for parents
to remember the child they lost, even if by miscarriage. SHARE
at St. John's Hospital in Springfield, Illinois, encourages parents
to give themselves keepsakes and to invent rituals to help them
actualize their grief.

Resolve, Inc., offers support groups for parents who struggle
with infertility. Often miscarriage victims are included, because
the definition of infertility includes the inability to carry pregnancy
to a live birth.

Resolve understands that people are often timid about reaching out for the kind of help their group specializes in because

often they are still hoping for a full-term pregnancy. While that hope is alive, they postpone seeking help, deciding that it isn't needed yet. However, Resolve feels that if you are experiencing infertility problems of any kind, you deserve support along with the best possible information about your medical situation and about the options available to you.

CHRISTIAN SUPPORT

Perhaps the most appreciated benefit of a support group is the genuine Christian love often found there. Many times it is a Christian who realizes the power that love has to heal who forms the group in the first place.

Dr. Russell Striffler, director of chaplaincy at St. Luke's Hospital in Cedar Rapids, Iowa, saw parents' need for support when they lost a fetus and, with a pediatric nurse clinician (who was also an active Christian), he developed the group that is now known as Support for Parents With Empty Arms. They began by writing letters to sixty couples. Those who responded have been meeting on a regular basis for more than six years. "We feel our efforts are a part of our Christian responsibility to care for all persons," Dr. Striffler wrote in a personal letter to me, "particularly those who have specific needs which neither the church nor medical personnel have met."[7]

Christina Hom, founder of Sacramento's Sharing Parents chapter, is also a Christian. So are many of her group members. "In the group," she says, "I'm a cheerleader for Christ. Being there gives us a chance to find hope in the midst of devastation and to share Christ with nonbelievers. They see that it's not that we don't grieve, but that [as Christians] we have *hope.*"

"The love of Christ gets in in subtle ways," says Kathy Johnson, another Christian Sharing Parents regular, "and the group reinforces what I'm hearing from the Lord — that I'm OK. I don't always hear that from Christians within the church."

The growth of support groups, often guided by the wisdom of God's own people, seems proof that this is something to which our Lord wants us to have access. Unfortunately, such groups don't exist in every town, but there is no reason they can't. Most support groups are formed through the initiative of parents and, while starting one requires an investment of time, energy and dedication that can be draining, it is a rewarding ministry.

If your community has no fetal loss support group, and you think you'd like to start one, don't feel that it's too overwhelming for you or that you aren't qualified. Christina knew nothing when she started. She was a Lamaze instructor who saw the need in the lives of her students when their babies died. She affiliated with SHARE and took off from there.

When Paula lost a baby in miscarriage, she attended Sharing Parents and found that she was the only member who had experienced an early fetal loss rather than a stillbirth. With Christina's help, she and her husband formed a special miscarriage group within the program. They began with only two or three parents attending but now the group has expanded and serves as an important part of the Sharing Parents ministry.

Mothers-In-Crisis in Joplin, Missouri, began with only three mothers who saw a need in their town and got help from the Freeman Hospital Social Services Department. The hospital department trained these mothers, gave them its endorsement, and the group was born. Since then, one group member has become a perinatal social worker and has been hired by the hospital to visit each family in the hospital immediately after a loss. She gives them support and information and invites them to the group meetings. Mothers-In-Crisis now exists in four states.

One Mothers-In-Crisis worker explains so much better than I can her reasons for participating: "I do so many things for my other children, and this is what I do for my baby who died."[8]

Should you decide to "go for it," you might want to begin by contacting one of these organizations:

Maureen Connelly
A.M.E.N.D.
4324 Berrywick Terrace
St. Louis, MO 63128

Phyllis Hardwick
The Compassionate Friends
P. O. Box 1347
Oak Brook, IL 60521

Rana Limbo
Resolve Through Sharing
LaCrosse Lutheran Hospital
1910 South Avenue
LaCrosse, WI 54601

Sister Jane Marie Lamb
SHARE
St. John's Hospital
800 East Carpenter
Springfield, IL 62762

P.E.P.D.
P. O. Box 38445
Germantown, TN 38138

As Christians, we know that one of God's greatest gifts to us is each other. Leading or participating in a support group is a special way to use that gift at a time when we need His richest blessings the most.

PART FIVE

Where Do We Go From Here?

> Now when Jesus heard it, He withdrew from there in a boat, to a lonely place by Himself; and when the multitudes heard of this, they followed Him on foot from the cities.
>
> And when He came out, He saw a great multitude and felt compassion for them, and healed their sick.
>
> Matthew 14:13-15

FIFTEEN

What Is Our Childbearing Future?

"So what are you going to do now?" Dr. Breeden asked me when I saw him four weeks after my miscarriage. "Back to birth control or try again?"

I looked at him helplessly and shrugged.

For weeks I'd thought about little else. Losing William Bradley made me realize how much I did want another child. It was still *him* I longed to hold and coo over, but it seemed to me that another pregnancy right away would help ease the ache of loss.

However, Jim was already considering having a vasectomy, and the idea of "fighting" for another baby didn't appeal to me. We'd shared Marijean with such joy. I couldn't imagine having a child my husband didn't want.

HASTY DECISION

With the lack of communication that was characteristic of our marriage at that point, we didn't discuss our real feelings. We talked more about the practical realities involved in having another child. In the end, I gave in to my need to do *something*, and we signed the papers for the vasectomy. It was the biggest mistake either of us ever made.

Our family doctor tried to talk us out of it, reminding us that we had only one child, that I was only thirty-one years old, and that a vasectomy couldn't necessarily be reversed should we change our minds.

But we went ahead with it, and I didn't shed a tear. I deliberately focused on the future and the fulfillment I planned to find in a new job. I stacked a hasty decision on top of unresolved grief and got on with my life, not knowing I was headed for real trouble.

Eighteen months later, when all our feelings erupted, the anger, guilt, sadness and disappointment that lay between us churned out in an ugly brew that bordered on hate. It took a very long time for us to wade through the bitterness and resentment and rebuild our relationship.

When finally our relationship was back in focus, we dealt openly with the issue of having another baby. We did want a second child, but now it simply wasn't that easy.

Our doctor resisted the temptation to say, "I told you so," and gave us the names of hospitals that might attempt a reversal. But the price tag was approximately $6,000, and there was no guarantee of success.

By then I was nearly thirty-three and not known for conceiving easily. Even if we could afford a reversal of the vasectomy, and even if it were successful, I might not become pregnant before I passed into the high-risk zone for having a baby. The biological time clock was ticking much too fast, and just then, neither one of us was completely sure that we weren't just trying to patch things up between us by each giving in to the other's desire to have a baby.

So, rather than pursue adoption or take out a second mortgage on the house to pay for an operation, we decided to turn the matter of a second child over to the Lord. Prayer, meditation and quiet perusal of Scripture did bring answers in time.

PARENTAL ROLES

Jim and I have a strong marriage now, born out of a new honesty with each other and the teamwork we share as Marijean's parents.

Together we act as advisors for a group of thirteen energetic Christian teenagers who hug our necks and call us at midnight for advice and tell us we're a great "Mom and Dad." They fill a need we both have to share our love with young people.

We've taken on a financial commitment to a child in Thailand whom we love and support by sending letters and pictures along with the money for his care.

The easy fit of these parental roles assures me that this is the place we need to be now. But it seems the future may hold even more.

Recently in a movie theater, we encountered a little Korean boy who stole both our hearts. Almost simultaneously we began to talk about adopting a foreign child, a four- or five-year-old rather than a baby, a little person we could raise.

"I'd love it," Jim said. He had tears in his eyes, and so did I. Maybe we were crying for the son we never had a chance to take to the movies. Perhaps we wept for the option to have other children that we no longer enjoyed. But I think our tears were tears of joy — that we finally came together in the choice our God wanted us to make all along.

Jim and I made the mistakes we did because we didn't know what to do. Many couples find themselves in that position after a pregnancy loss. The questions about their future as parents come at them thick and fast, from without as well as from within.

"Get pregnant right away," some people say. "Before you know it, you'll have a new baby in your arms, and you'll forget how much this hurts."

"Don't have another one too soon," others say. "You've been through so much."

The advice never stops coming: "Why chance it? Adopt a baby!" Or, "What do you want to have kids for anyway? What about your career?"

As they sift through well-meant advice, bereaved parents often find themselves disagreeing with *each other.*

Husbands may hesitate to "try again" immediately, either because they don't want to risk seeing their wives suffer another loss, or because they haven't resolved their own grief. However, some men see no need to wait, because they didn't feel the loss of the baby as intensely as their wives did. Or they may want another baby because they feel it will ease their wives' depression.

Some mothers also want to rush to conceive again, either to alleviate their pain or to fulfill the need to hold their own baby in their arms. Yet others pull back from their husbands' eagerness to try for pregnancy immediately; they fear another heartbreak or are still in too much emotional pain to think of anything but the baby they lost.

CAREFUL DECISIONS

There are two important points I stress with anyone who recently has been a victim of miscarriage. (Doctors and counselors — as well as my own experience — back up the crucial nature of this advice):

(1) *Avoid making permanent decisions that can't be reversed.* Big changes in your lives that can't be undone are best postponed until you've resolved your grief and sorted through your feelings. It's tempting to make drastic changes when you're suffering because the act seems to ease the pain and helplessness you feel.

But the restlessness will chase you until your grief is resolved. Why take steps you may not be able to retrace? Let the disappointment and fear that blind you from objective decision-making fade before you make new choices. As Kreis and Pattie advise in *Up From Grief,* "In grieving, leave future plans to the future. You aren't ready for major decisions."[1]

(2) When you *are* ready, *seek God's will together* as husband and wife to discover what is best to do next for your family. That involves sorting out your desires and feelings *and* finding out what God wants for you. Remember, you're making a decision that may affect the rest of your life. Don't base it merely on how you feel today.

Pray together. Sort out your feelings and express them honestly to each other. Then trust God's guidance in whatever comes. As Maureen Rank writes in *Free to Grieve,* "It's enough that He's there, whether you get what *you* want or not." He always meets the true needs we have.[2]

The marvelous thing about God is that He does give us a mind to use to make choices that coincide with His desires for us. Deciding whether or not to try for pregnancy after a miscarriage occurs can be especially difficult as it involves so many variables.

WHEN TO TRY AGAIN

The only danger a couple faces when they choose to try for pregnancy again is to do it for the wrong reasons: to create a stand-in for the lost baby, or to escape the pain of his death. Having another baby immediately isn't the route to comfort. "Grief," says Dr. James Robinson, "rejects all substitutes."[3]

The key to a healthy approach seems to be in deciding *when* it's time to conceive again. Doctors advise waiting three months to give your body ample time for recovery. This gives the mother time to return to a regular cycle of ovulation and menstruation, and allows her hormones to settle into normalcy once more. Some physicians say this also gives enough time for the formation of a healthy inner lining of the uterus.

A couple also should recover emotionally from their loss before deciding to conceive again. The amount of time this takes varies from couple to couple. Ann waited three years before becoming pregnant again, and then gave birth to Richard. "I didn't want to face the possibility of another failure any sooner," she says ruefully.

Lynda was anxious to become pregnant again immediately and, against the advice of her doctor, conceived six weeks after her miscarriage. The pregnancy was a rocky one, plagued by bleeding and high blood pressure problems. When spotting started at three months, she feared she couldn't deal with another loss.

As it turned out, she didn't have to. But when Allison was born at seven and a half months and had to remain in neonatal intensive care for several weeks after Lynda was discharged, Lynda became depressed. She suffered panic, obsessive thoughts, and sleepless nights for almost a year. Only after Allison reached her first birthday did Lynda resolve the grief over her lost baby and accept the fact that her daughter was going to live a healthy life.

You'll know it's time to try to have another baby when:

- you realize you want one for what you can share with him or her;
- you feel it's what God wants in your life;
- you know you can accept whatever happens in the pregnancy;
- you know you've done all you can physically and emotionally to be ready.

The following questions have been suggested by Resolve Through Sharing to help you discover how ready you are to conceive again. Ask them of yourself, and try to answer them honestly.

- Does the loss still consume all my thoughts?
- Am I obsessed with becoming pregnant?
- Can I think about the loss without it tearing me apart?
- Am I able once again to find importance in other people and activities?
- Do I have happiness in my life, so that I can laugh and

enjoy myself?
- Am I expecting this next child to make me feel better?

Answers that indicate a readiness to conceive again express acceptance of your previous loss, enjoyment of life, friends and marriage, and anticipation of another baby for its own sake.

WHAT ARE OUR CHANCES?

Normal delivery of a healthy infant occurs for about 80 percent of the women who have had one previous miscarriage and 60 percent of those who have had two.[4] Even after several miscarriages, a baby that is finally carried to term is more likely to be normal because the mother's body has a proven mechanism for rejecting abnormalities.[5]

But your chances of delivering a normal child depend not so much on the number of miscarriages you've had as on how you answer these questions:

Was the fetus you lost chromosomally abnormal? If so, it probably happened by chance, and your next baby will most likely be full-term and healthy. If it did not happen by chance, other medical factors may be involved which may (or may not) endanger your next pregnancy.

Have you given birth to other children? If so, you know your system can work and probably will work again.

WHILE YOU WAIT

The months of waiting for another pregnancy can be torturous, but here are some things you can do in the interim:

(1) *Schedule a complete physical,* just to be sure there are no systemic or structural problems that may hinder your next pregnancy. If you've had more than one miscarriage, have an endocrine study done to check for problems that might be treated with hormone therapy.
(2) *If you're overweight or underweight, get nutritional counseling.* Women at either end of the weight spectrum run a higher risk of miscarrying than others.
(3) *Avoid exposure to harmful substances.* Exposure before conception as well as during pregnancy can increase the chances of miscarriage or birth defects.
(4) *Use birth control to give yourself peace of mind as you wait.* Preventing conception during the wait between pregnancies

is a subject that worries many Christians. They may fear the ramifications of birth control or feel it's against God's will not to "let nature take its course."

A few words from Walter Trobisch, author of *A Christian View of Contraception*, may ease any worries you have. He reasons that our physical life is entrusted to us by God. We are responsible for our bodies and for our children. Why did God give us brains, he asserts, if not to draw conclusions and use the gifts of science (contraceptives) for proper ends?[6]

I agree with him. As a parent you will want to be physically and emotionally ready to give your next child all the love he needs. If using birth control for a few months gives you the time to prepare for that, so be it.

GETTING THROUGH ANOTHER PREGNANCY

Sixty percent of couples who try to conceive again are successful by the sixth month, and another 30 percent go on to conceive within a year.[7] But it often surprises them that the new pregnancy doesn't necessarily "make everything OK again."

While the previous pregnancy may have been filled with joy and anticipation from the outset, this one probably will be tinged with fear.

Some mothers find it hard to accept the next pregnancy as a reality, and they either want repeated tests to prove it or they refuse prenatal care for awhile.

Others become overly cautious, some to the point of giving up physical exercise and sex during the pregnancy "just to be on the safe side."

If the miscarriage was painful, the mother may be afraid that a live birth will be absolutely unbearable.

It's also common for a woman to put off making any plans for the baby or even forming an attachment to him. If they have no other children, the mother and father may not prepare themselves emotionally or mentally to be parents for fear they'll become too attached to the baby and then lose him.

Until they've passed the point in the pregnancy at which they lost their last baby, both parents may require constant reassurance, and may spend hours talking anxiously to each other or calling the obstetrician.

All of that can be expected. Where once pregnancy was thought of as a carefree, beautiful time, it's now a period laced with anxiety. But here are some things an expectant mother and father can do to ease their fears so as not to miss the joys of pregnancy:

(1) *Chase away negative thoughts* like *I'll probably lose this one, too,* or, *What if he lives and has some terrible birth defect?* Your mind can't hold two thoughts at once, so when the fearful ones slip in, replace them immediately with positive statements: "I've done everything I can do. God is going to take care of the rest." "I love this baby. I am a good mother." Write those affirmations down if you have to, or say them out loud, but use them. They'll allow you to form the bond with your baby that pessimism renders impossible.

(2) *Find passages of Scripture that comfort you, and read them often.* The power of God's Word is awesome.

(3) *As each new situation arises, look at it honestly rather than pessimistically or hysterically.* If you can't reassure yourself, call your doctor. You're paying him and his staff to make your pregnancy as comfortable as possible, and that includes a relaxed mental state! Remember, too, that high risk pregnancies can be monitored closely and some problems can be treated immediately. There's no reason to give up hope when trouble stirs.

(4) *Find someone you can talk to,* someone who understands your fears and who won't say, "Oh, for Pete's sake, relax!" Someone who has been where you are is probably your best bet. Don't forget that our Lord understands, too. Talk to Him often. If severe anxiety or panic interferes with your life so that you can't sleep, can't concentrate or can't relax, or to the extent that you withdraw from everyone, seek professional counseling. There's no shame in that, and it will be the best thing for you, your family and your unborn baby.

(5) *Enroll early in a prenatal class.* Use your instructor as part of your support system.

(6) *Don't refrain from sex* as a precaution during your pregnancy unless your doctor advises it. Orgasm doesn't lead to labor. Minimal spotting after intercourse isn't harmful. The baby is well protected by the cervix, the mucous plug and the membranes. Abstinence only robs you of the closeness you need.

(7) If your age or other circumstances make you feel you can't wait, and you become pregnant again before you've resolved your grief, *let the new pregnancy BE a new pregnancy.* Let this baby be somebody different from the baby who died. Be conscious of what's going on emotionally and take the time during your pregnancy to grieve for your other baby.

(8) *Take comfort in the fact that your miscarriage was probably*

more painful than what you'll experience as you give birth to a healthy full-term baby. The contractions of a miscarriage are more like severe cramps or spasms than like the rhythmic, wave-like tightening and relaxation you experience in healthy labor. Miscarriage pains are hard to anticipate, and their intensity is increased by the mother's tension and fear.[8] When it's time for you to deliver your healthy baby, you probably will have the back-up experience of childbirth preparation classes to keep you calm and in control. This will be an entirely different experience and not one to dread.

(9) Don't be alarmed if it takes you longer than you expected to bond with your baby after birth or if you feel uneasy about his safety in infancy. These are normal reactions, and with prayer, time and your baby's wonderful toothless smiles, you'll grow past them.

WHEN YOU'VE LOST MORE THAN ONE BABY

Simple solutions are difficult for the family who has suffered more than one miscarriage.

If the losses have been "late" spontaneous abortions, occurring between seventeen and twenty-eight weeks of pregnancy, the cause is often a mystery, and the chances of having another loss after you've had two goes up to 33 percent. After three such losses, the chances of having a fourth rise to 50 percent.[9] Needless to say, with subsequent pregnancies a woman can be haunted by fears.

Branded with the unfortunate label of "habitual aborter," a mother who tries unsuccessfully to give birth again and again and loses her pregnancies early can doubt whether she's ever going to have a healthy baby.

Kathy Johnson had two healthy boys with no problems, but her next four pregnancies ended in miscarriage, all within eighteen months. Two months after her last miscarriage, she was still shaky. "I don't want to go through this any more," she said. "I don't want to go through the grief. I don't want to face any more anniversary dates [of the babies' deaths]. I just want to shut down. I'm tired of the emotional yo-yo. I'm tired of what it's doing to my family, and the fact that it doesn't stop. I quit! It can stop; I'm ready to get off — and yet I can't. I'm really frustrated, because we do want another baby so much."

Kathy underwent extensive testing that revealed no cause for her repeated losses, something that happens in 85 percent of habitual abortion cases. "I'd be willing to be sick if I could just have a reason for all this death," she says. "I can't think of anything else to throw out of my diet or my lifestyle! I'd like to get pregnant Thursday, go into labor Friday and have the baby Saturday! The thought of another two, or three — or nine — months of insanity scares me."

After a long period of infertility, Anne and Joe suffered two miscarriages before having a healthy baby girl. Although that pregnancy was problem-free, the next five ended in miscarriage, and her pregnancy with twins brought only one baby boy to term alive. There were two more miscarriages after that.

"Each time, I hated to go to the doctor. With my last child I decided I wasn't going to go in until it was time to deliver, and then I'd just show up and say, 'Here I am!' But I didn't. Each time I got pregnant I was afraid to go to the bathroom because I was afraid I'd see spotting."

Anne's losses are the result of a translocation (a genetic defect in either the egg or sperm), and an inadequate initial phase, which robs the uterus of sufficient hormones to prepare itself for implantation of the fertilized egg. Chance determines whether she loses a baby in the first trimester, and after that, hormone shots are necessary for her to keep the pregnancy.

"My only hope is that I've done it before so I can do it again. Something went right twice, so I know it can work. That's what I hold on to."

Being pregnant after two or more miscarriages is so formidable a situation that it seems only faith and the support of family and friends can carry a mother through. Most who have done it strongly urge couples to insist on testing before waiting longer to become pregnant. While a cause for the losses reveals itself in only 15 percent of the cases, the feeling that you've done everything you can may be enough to carry you through.

While many doctors insist on a history of three losses before testing is done, you can assert yourself and have tests done when *you* feel it's time. Waiting to lose three babies can be torturous.

Although no one specializes in habitual abortion per se, many obstetricians and gynecologists specialize in high-risk pregnancy or infertility. The testing done under their care can be a tedious, trying experience. Pat reported three months of intensive lab tests that drained her of energy. One month she visited the doctor's office, the hospital or the lab on fifteen of the twenty working days. "And so often through the whole thing, the medical people would say to me in one way or another, 'Do you have some kind of emotional problem that makes you put yourself through this? Why don't you give up?'"

The tests may not reveal why your pregnancies continue to end in miscarriage. However, even after three or more miscarriages, statistics show that you still have a 70 percent chance of carrying a baby to term, with or without any kind of treatment. Educate yourself, and you'll know you did everything possible. It will be so much easier then to turn your situation over to God.

AFTER AN ECTOPIC PREGNANCY

Entrusting herself to God may be exactly what the victim of an ectopic pregnancy should do. (You'll remember that an ectopic pregnancy occurs when the fertilized egg implants somewhere other than in the uterus, and most often in the Fallopian tube.) Only 50 percent of the women who've had one ectopic pregnancy become pregnant again, and 7 to 12 percent of these have another ectopic, since whatever may have caused the egg to nest in one Fallopian tube may also have affected the other.[10] The waiting that begins after another conception involves not only wondering if this baby will make it, but whether or not you will escape death again, and if you will lose your ability to have children with this pregnancy.

"The end of the childbearing years is sad in itself for some people," says Kathleen Bernau, M.S.N. at Rose Medical Center, "but having the decision possibly taken out of your hands makes it more difficult."[11]

IF YOU HAVE A HISTORY OF INFERTILITY

Infertility due to ectopic pregnancies or miscarriages, called *secondary infertility,* can be frustrating and baffling. Not only are you suffering the loss of a much-wanted child, but you face an obstacle in your desire to have another one. The admonition, "Don't worry; you conceived once. You'll be able to do it again," offers little comfort, because you're not sure you'll ever become pregnant again, or how long it will take.

If you are past thirty, you may feel time's winged chariot at your back and you may try to conceive before you've had a chance to grieve the loss of your baby. You may easily become obsessed with conception, living from one menstrual period to the next in an agony of anticipation and fear. You may become terrified that your own anxiety keeps you from getting pregnant.

Here are some suggestions given by parents I've talked with who also have suffered through periods of infertility:

(1) *Remember, it's highly unlikely that anxiety prevents pregnancy.* Don't browbeat yourself into thinking that your own "craziness" is keeping you from conceiving.

(2) *Seek the help of a support group designed especially for you.* Resolve, Inc., has chapters in almost every major city and town in the United States.

(3) *Study all your options.* You can see a specialist, undergo testing, and take steps to improve your chances of conceiving. You can begin to release your inability to have children and to look for other ways to satisfy your intense need to share your love with a child. You can start looking into the possibility of adopting, since that procedure is also time-consuming.

(4) *Look to the Lord.* He hurts for you, and He knows how to help you. But you have to go to Him and lay your situation before Him.

WHEN DO YOU STOP TRYING?

When do you stop trying to conceive? is a question that only you can answer. You'll need to take an honest look at your medical condition, make an appraisal of your emotional state, measure the intensity of your feelings and do a thorough search for God's will. Adding it all up should point you to your decision as to whether you keep trying or you look at other options.

And there *are* other options. People say it's difficult to adopt, yet every day couples bring home children who were adopted through agencies or privately. Why shouldn't you be one of the lucky ones if you want children? Ann Kiemel Anderson, author of *Taste of Tears — Touch of God*, prayed through insurmountable obstacles and odds and is now the adoptive mother of Taylor Jenkins Anderson.

She writes:

> because life is a miracle
> because we waited so long
> because we are so overjoyed
> because God did it . . .
> we celebrate![12]

If you don't want to adopt or are unable to, you'll go through the painful process of adjusting to a life without children or with fewer children than you had hoped for. That can be tough, but there are options here, too. You can still love and have contact with children. You can change your ideas about what makes "a family." And most important of all, you can *decide* that you are no less a woman simply because you aren't a mother of six or no less a man because you don't have a brood of heirs.

"A woman," writes Walter Trobisch, "is not essentially a womb, a sort of well-equipped incubator. Parenthood is a free gift of God's goodness, but childlessness is no shame."[13]

If anyone feels bleak, guilty and helpless about a future with no more children in their lives, it might be Jim and me.

But we don't feel any of those things. We did what we thought was right at the time, without benefit of the strength and wisdom we have now. We can deal with our choices. We can go on, knowing we made mistakes. Because of the Lord's hand in our lives, we are a family now . . . and perhaps we will be even more of a family in days to come.

SIXTEEN

Can I Make My Loss A Ministry?

About a month before I learned I was pregnant with William Bradley, one of my students discovered she was expecting a baby.

Rosa was a beautiful Mexican girl with honey-colored skin, brown velvet eyes and a rich tumble of black curls. Everything about her was tenderness itself. I was sure she would be a fine mother, even though she was only sixteen and she and her husband Francisco had been married only six months and had very little money.

During the time that I was pregnant, we shared a special friendship. We compared tummies, yawned in tune over the afternoon sleepies and commiserated over morning nausea. It was as if we shared a secret no one else knew.

But when I returned to work after my miscarriage, Rosa was cool and aloof. She slipped into the classroom late, carefully avoided my eyes and buried herself in her books until the end of each session, when she scurried out of the room as if I were chasing her.

NEEDED

It didn't take me long to realize that Rosa was terrified that her baby was going to die, too, and that somehow being around me was dangerous. My suddenly flat stomach was a grim reminder that that loss was a possibility.

One day she finally looked at me straight on, her eyes swimming with terror. Beautiful and poised and mature as she was in her Madonna-like state, the fear on her face reminded me that she was really just a child, a baby having a baby. She needed someone to hug her and reassure her that she and her butterscotch-colored little one were going to be just fine. She needed that someone to be me.

I took her hand and led her out into the hall where I put my arms around her and whispered to her, "This isn't going to happen to your baby. You two are going to be just great."

Her face broke into smiles, and she locked both arms around my neck. As I stood there holding her round little body, I prayed that it would be true.

That wasn't all she needed from me, though. With her delivery only four months away, there was much to be done.

She needed several credits in order to graduate in May, and we immediately went to work on them.

For English she researched breast versus bottle feeding, Lamaze versus LaBoye, Spock versus Brazleton. For science we worked out a balanced diet and she studied the stages of fetal development.

For math I guided her in setting up a budget, balancing her checkbook, and analyzing ways for her and Francisco to pay their upcoming hospital bills.

She was concerned also about how they were going to handle their responsibilities as new parents. We spent many lunch hours together talking about the changes she was about to face. I loaned her several books on child care and helped her find a parent education class.

When little Francisco made his appearance in early May, Rosa was ready. The nursery was set up, the bills were paid, and her mind was in accord with her husband's on how they planned to raise their new son. Just a few days before he was born, Rosa took her last test in my class. She graduated from high school in June, with little Francisco and me in the audience, both crying our eyes out.

At times, it was almost impossible for me to deal with the jealousy I felt toward Rosa and her good fortune, to love her when my inclination was to hate. It was hard to look at her steadily blossoming tummy while mine remained flaccid and empty. It was difficult to help her make plans when all of mine had been dashed. It was tough to reach out when all I wanted to do was nurse my own wounds.

But if I did anything right in those first months after William's death, being there for Rosa was it. Because of my anxiety, I could understand her fear and help her overcome it. Knowing what it was to lose, I wanted so much to see her win, and I did.

HELPING OTHERS

Much later, while reading the Bible one morning, I came across a portion of Matthew's Gospel where he tells us that when Jesus learned of John the Baptist's death, He went to a lonely place to mourn. He must have grieved very deeply; John was someone He loved dearly, and the fact that he died so suddenly and violently must have shaken our Lord into the full realization of how the end was going to be for Him.

However, He didn't hide Himself long. As soon as the crowds heard where He was, they left the towns and went after Him, hungry for both physical and spiritual food. The disciples would have sent them away, but even in His grief, Jesus insisted they be fed, and He performed the necessary miracle to see that they didn't go away hungry (Matthew 14:13-21).

Jesus took a few precious moments to be alone, to mourn and to pray. He saw the need to withdraw into His sorrow for a short while, but then He knew He must return to His ministry to others.[1]

So it should be for us. To stop at personal recovery is to ignore the example Christ set. Once you've mourned, you need to return to helping others, using what you now know, not only intellectually but also through experience.

Your ministry can take form through your responses to people who suffer any kind of hurt, as you tell them it's OK to *feel.* As you reach out for them, touch them and tell them you care.

Since I faced my grief over William's death and grew to recovery, I've found myself on a silent mission to help people when they hurt. Because I've suffered, too, I seem to know just how to do it, and I can't imagine refraining from sharing that new wealth.

One friend was facing a frightening court battle that could have put him in prison, and I knew it was appropriate to drop in on him in the late afternoons when he felt especially down. I knew it was important to just listen while he poured out his bitterness, and I knew not to reproach him when he lashed out at God.

When another friend underwent a hysterectomy, I went to her and listened while she cried because she couldn't have more children. She was forty-five. She had a son and a wonderful husband. Several years before, I would have reminded her of all she had and told her she ought to look at the bright side. But I know what it's like to lose your ability to give birth, no matter what the circumstances, so I let her cry, and I cried with her.

When anyone seems ready to take the Lord into their lives, I show them how, and I pray with them and for them, and I talk to them about the incredible things Christ can do. There was a time when I was a "closet Christian" and, frankly, the idea of witnessing turned me off. But now that I've faced the pit of despair with no one to turn to but God, and given all my fears to Him, I know it's the only way, and I know it's my job to spread the word. Not to do so would be like discovering a cure for cancer and saving it for only myself.

The ministry that grows from loss also can be a more formal, purposeful one.

SPECIFIC MINISTRIES

Established support groups are hungry for new facilitators and trained counselors who have experienced a pregnancy loss. New support groups are desperately needed in places where no network for grieving parents exists.

After Mary Wasacz's baby daughter died, she and her family realized that their spiritual healing from grief had been a miracle, one they wanted to share with other bereaved parents. They began a hot line that grew into the Infant Bereavement Group of Scarsdale, New York. Mary went on to be trained as a family therapist and is now in private practice.

Anne, a busy dentist with her own practice, takes phone calls from miscarriage victims during working hours. "I provide a shared experience," she says. "People trust me enough to pour out their innermost thoughts and feelings over the phone, because they know I won't judge."

Newsletters need your written personal experiences, poems and essays to comfort and bolster mothers and fathers suffering fresh pain. Hospitals need volunteers. So do crisis pregnancy centers, hot lines, and organizations that raise money to fight birth defects.

A specific ministry may find its niche in the church. In fact, that's exactly where one ought to begin. Jesus' death for us washed away our sin, but it didn't end the physical and emotional pain we experience on earth. The church exists as a community for those who suffer, and those of us who have known pain can help end the isolation so many others feel. Through the cross of Christ we can help fellow Christians come to terms with suffering.[2]

Kathy Johnson's heartbreaking series of losses nudged her pastor to begin a church program to teach people how to comfort those who suffer or grieve. "He realizes," says Kathy, "that the reason the church isn't meeting people's needs is that it doesn't know how." Kathy and her husband are playing a key role in helping implement the program.

Both Pat and Anne and their husbands help facilitate "comfort study groups" in their respective churches. Lynda taught an adult Sunday school class to help young couples face the struggles of marriage and family life, including the problems of childbearing and child rearing, depression and spiritual conflicts. We have an obligation to minister from our experience in the church community; we can't expect our pastors to know it all.

THIS BOOK

The book you hold in your hands is the most obvious example of my formal ministry. At first, I researched the facts you found in the early chapters for my own benefit. After a few months of frenzied study, I found some satisfaction, and I tucked the information into a drawer.

Two years later when my life began to come together again, Jim prodded me. "Whatever happened to all that stuff on miscarriage?" he asked.

"It's in there," I said vaguely.

"Aren't you going to do anything with it?"

"Like what?" I said.

"Weren't you going to write a book?"

I just shrugged.

"What good is it doing anybody else when it's stuck in a drawer?" he demanded. "I think you ought to get it out. It could help somebody."

So I did. There was a lot of work to do, of course. And even if I did bring it up to date, and wrote a book proposal, and found a publisher, what if it never was purchased or read?

Was I wasting my time?

I pursued it anyway, and a few weeks after I submitted my outline and sample chapters to Here's Life Publishers, my phone rang. It wasn't the publisher offering me a magnificent advance and telling me I was the next Charles Swindoll — it was a woman on the staff who'd been asked to review my proposal.

"I just finished reading your two chapters," she said. Her voice sounded strange, as if she were on the verge of tears. "I had a miscarriage myself a few years ago, and your book made me realize I haven't really . . ." Her voice broke. Suddenly she was crying on my shoulder from a thousand miles away.

We talked for two hours. I listened as she told her story and with it came the anger, the guilt, the pain, and the unresolved grief. When we hung up, driven only by the fear that she might have to take out a second mortgage on her house to pay for the call, she was laughing and wishing me God's blessings. I felt as if we were sisters.

"OK, OK, you were right," I said to Jim as I hung up. "It never would have done anybody any good stuck in a drawer."

He just smiled. We both knew that even if *Handling the Heartbreak of Miscarriage* never got into the hands of another reader, it had helped one person, and that was reason enough to have done it.

Whatever your talents, abilities, or motivations, I think the Lord has a job opening for you that you're well-prepared for. God gave you on-the-job training by comforting you so that now you know how to comfort others (2 Corinthians 1:8-11).

Kreis and Pattie, in their book *Up From Grief*, suggest that when someone important in your life dies, you are left with an untapped reservoir of love.[3] Letting *it* die, too, seems a sin.

"There's no higher calling than that God should use our suffering to be a help to others," writes Warren Wiersbe, author of *Why Us? When Bad Things Happen to God's People*.[4] What happens in us, he says, should help determine what happens through us.[5]

JESUS' EXAMPLE

Again, the precedent has been established by Christ Himself, who always sets the best example.

The child who grew in Mary's womb was no figment of her imagination. From the moment Gabriel made his famous announcement, Jesus developed in the amniotic sac just as any other child does. And when He was born, He probably experienced as much diaper rash and colic, as many skinned knees and runny noses, as any other kid. He grew up tasting, touching and crying just as we have done. He *felt* the nails being driven through His flesh precisely as we would have if it had happened to us.

If He were going to be man's savior, He had to have "been there." In the same way, we must experience our own pain before we can help someone else deal with theirs. "To be anyone's savior takes having been there,"[6] writes the anonymous author of "Forward Day by Day." You've lost a baby, and you know the special kind of grief a family suffers in that situation. Now you can minister as Jesus did.

But that doesn't mean just feeling compassion for others as they experience loss and the accompanying grief. Christ didn't just come among us, nod and say, "Wow! I see what you mean. This is the pits."

Not only did He live — up to his eyebrows — in the human condition, but He also did something about it by dying on the cross and rising out of the tomb.

You can do something, too — something meaningful in the lives of the people you know. You can touch them by caring and by sharing your experience with grief, because now you know what it means to hurt — and to be healed.

EPILOGUE

My life today is a full, rich, satisfying one, so much different from the one I led before my baby died.

That doesn't mean I'm glad I had a miscarriage. If William Bradley had lived, he'd be helping right now with Thanksgiving preparations. Marijean would be teaching him how to make a picture of a turkey out of the outline of his chubby hand, and there would be three of us gluing construction paper feathers to pine cones and licking the beaters from the pumpkin pie. I would have loved that, and sometimes I still long for it.

It also doesn't mean that everything I am now is a result of what happened to me then. But suffering the loss of our baby son was certainly a catalyst. It forced me to face my feelings at last with the respect they deserved. It coaxed me to reach out in honesty to other people and to turn to God as I'd never done before. I had no other choice. I had to do those things in order to survive.

With those lessons learned, I can no longer hide what I have to offer others, afraid of what they will think. I do have something to give them, and I venture forth every chance I get.

Thank you for picking up this book and giving me a chance to share my lessons with you. I hope it has helped you in some way, perhaps with information you needed to erase your guilt, maybe with shared experiences that have assured you that you're not alone in your grief, or perhaps with the reassurance that our Lord can work miracles of spiritual healing in your life the way He did in mine.

As I go, let me leave you with one more thought. You and your family have known a personal, quiet kind of loss that will be silently with you always. At times it might hurt again, and you may even cry. But you'll know these things for sure:

- With God at your side you're stronger and wiser and better than ever before.
- Now you can touch people in a way no one else can.
- And your baby? He's cradled in God's loving arms.

God bless you.

150

APPENDIX I

Normal Pregnancy

1. In the first half of a woman's menstrual cycle, her body hormones shift, causing an egg to ripen in one ovary. As it ripens, it moves to the outer surface of the ovary. When ovulation occurs, a surge of hormones thrusts the egg out of the ovary.

2. A man's semen (fluid discharged during intercourse) carries the guppy-like sperm. During intercourse, the penis is inserted into the vagina and sperm are released. Sperm move through the vagina, through the cervix (the opening to the uterus) and through the uterus to the Fallopian tubes.

3. After bursting forth from the ovary, the egg travels down a Fallopian tube toward the uterus. The sperm and egg meet, and one sperm penetrates the egg, thus fertilizing it.

4. Every month, hormonal changes prepare the lining of the uterus, the endometrium, to receive and nourish a fertilized egg. If no fertilized egg appears, the endometrium is shed in the monthly menstrual flow.

5. When conception occurs, the fertilized egg (called the embryo until the eighth week of pregnancy) travels down the Fallopian tube and plants itself in the endometrium. This process takes about seven or eight days after the egg has been fertilized. Some women experience slight implantation bleeding at this point.

6. A small cyst forms on the ovary where the egg first developed. This cyst produces a hormone called progesterone that sustains the pregnancy in the early weeks until the placenta has developed fully enough to take over.

7. Snuggled cozily in the endometrium, the fertilized egg cells divide. The endometrium thickens with enlarged blood vessels to nourish the growing fetus.

8. The placenta, which becomes the connecting organ between mother and baby, grows. It brings nourishment to the fetus and takes away waste.

APPENDIX II

Symptoms of a Miscarriage

1. Vaginal bleeding. The flow may be heavy and gushing or may be limited to scanty spotting that lasts several weeks.

2. Passing of fetal tissue. Fluffy discharge is from the placenta; tan-colored discharge is from the fetus. It's highly unlikely that a fully formed fetus will be discernable.

3. Pain. There may be slight cramping, a "something is wrong" sensation, a low backache, pelvic pressure, dull midline discomfort, knife-like pains or heavy contractions that resemble labor pains.

4. Nausea. Expect more than what you experience as the usual morning sickness.

5. Unusual fatigue.

Physical Problems in the Mother Which May Cause Pregnancy Loss

1. Irregularities in the shape of the uterus. These occur during the fetal development in 1 of 700 women. (They can be corrected surgically.)

2. Asherman's syndrome. This problem is recognizable by adhesions inside the uterus that form as a result of a previous D & C. (It can be corrected surgically.)

3. Fibroid tumors (myomas). (Although these may form in the uterus, it still may be possible to carry a baby to term — depending on the location of the myomas.)

4. Mothers who were DES babies. Diethylstilbestrol (DES) is a medication that was sometimes given to women in the 1940s and 1950s to prevent miscarriage. It altered the reproductive tracts of many of the women's female babies.

5. Early degeneration of the corpus luteum. This send-off spot on the ovary from which the egg is expelled can disintegrate before it produces sufficient progesterone to prepare the lining of the uterus for implantation. If the time span between ovulation and menstruation is short, the corpus will degenerate after only four or five days, before the lining of the uterus is prepared adequately. (Low dosages of certain fertility drugs can treat this condition.)

6. Blood incompatibilities. This condition is implicated in couples when the woman has Rh negative blood or a history that follows this course: first, one normal pregnancy; then a jaundiced baby; and then recurrent miscarriages at earlier and earlier stages.

7. An incompetent cervix. This factor occurs only in second trimester miscarriages. The cervix collapses under the increasing weight of the fetus and fluid. The condition may be caused by a weak cervical ring (a congenital defect), or previous damage to the cervix caused by a difficult vaginal birth, or one of several medical procedures (though that's unusual). (It can be repaired with surgery.)

8. Viruses and infections. Rubella, cytomegalovirus (CMV) and herpes simplex are potential causes of miscarriage. Women with herpes have a fetal loss rate three times higher than normal. (These can be treated with antibiotics before

the next pregnancy.)

9. Health problems. Peritonitis, hepatitis, chicken pox, mumps, hypertension, diabetes, tumors, acute infections, endometriosis, anemia, pneumonia, active bowel disease and cancer are each suspected, but not proven, causes of miscarriage.

10. Immunological abnormality. In this condition the mother lacks antibodies that apparently protect the baby from rejection as foreign tissue. It can provoke loss of a pregnancy. (The condition is called subclinical autoimmune disease and is not yet treatable.)

APPENDIX IV

Signals That Professional Counseling Is Needed

If, a year after a miscarriage (or any time span the individual honestly feels is too long), any of the following problems still persists, professional counseling is advised:

1. feelings that are still as intense as they were the day of the miscarriage;
2. a physical illness or condition which persists and cannot be diagnosed medically;
3. thoughts of suicide;
4. drastic weight change;
5. insomnia;
6. total self-induced isolation;
7. heavy use of drugs or alcohol;
8. continued absence of sexual desire;
9. chronic fatigue with no apparent physical cause;
10. fear of being alone.

APPENDIX V

Recommended Readings for Helping Children Deal With Death

FOR YOUNG CHILDREN:

Buscaglia, Leo. *The Fall of Freddie the Leaf.* Thorofare, NJ: Charles B. Slack, Inc., 1982.

Coburn, John B. *Anne and the Sand Dobbies: A Story About Death for Children and Their Parents.* New York: Seabury Press, 1964.

Dodge, N. and Veara, K. *Thumpy's Story.* Springfield, IL: Prairie Lark Press, 1984.

Mumford, Amy Ross, and Danhauer, Karen E. *Love Away My Hurt: A Child's Book About Death.* Denver: Accent Publications, 1983.

Nystrom, Carolyn. *What Happens When We Die?* Chicago: Moody Press, 1981.

Stein, Sara Bonnett. *About Dying.* New York: Walker & Co., 1974.

FOR OLDER CHILDREN:

Agee, James. *Death in the Family.* New York: Bantam, 1971.

Donovan, John. *Wild in the World.* New York: Harper & Row, 1971.

Garden, Nancy. *The Loners.* New York: Viking Press, 1972.

Klein, Norma. *Sunshine.* New York: Holt, Rinehart & Winston, 1975.

McHugh, Mary. *Young People Talk About Death.* Danbury, CT: Watts, Franklin, Inc., 1980.

Peck, Richard. *Dreamland Lake.* New York: Dell, 1982.

Woodford, Peggy. *Please Don't Go.* New York: Avon Books, 1975.

FOR PARENTS:

Grollman, Earl A. *Talking About Death: A Dialogue Between Parents and Child.* Boston: Beacon Press, 1970.

Rogers, F. *Talking With Young Children About Death.* Pittsburgh: Mr. Rogers' Neighborhood, Family Communications, 1979.

Rudolph, Marguerita. *Should the Children Know?* New York: Schocken Books, 1978.

Stellman, P. *Answers to a Child's Questions About Death.* Stamford, NY: Guidelines Pub., 1979.

NOTES

Chapter 1
    1. Rana Limbo and Sara Rich Wheeler, "Women's Responses to the Loss of Their Pregnancy Through Miscarriage: A Longitudinal Study" (M.A. thesis, LaCrosse Lutheran Hospital Nursing School, LaCrosse, WI, 1985), p. 1.
    2. Resolve Through Sharing, *Ectopic Pregnancy* (LaCrosse: LaCrosse Lutheran Hospital, 1984).

Chapter 3
    1. *Encyclopedia Britannica*, 1973 ed., s.v. "Pregnancy."
    2. Rochelle Friedman and Bonnie Gradstein, *Surviving Pregnancy Loss* (Boston: Little, Brown and Co., 1982), p. 24.
    3. Resolve Through Sharing, *Ectopic Pregnancy* (LaCrosse: LaCrosse Lutheran Hospital, 1984).
    4. Friedman and Gradstein, *Surviving Pregnancy Loss*, p. 35.
    5. Ibid.

Chapter 4
    1. William Kotzwinkle, *Swimmer in the Secret Sea* (New York: Avon Books, 1975), p. 74.
    2. Jane Brody, "The New and Often Reassuring Information About Miscarriage," *Redbook* (April 1983), p. 53.
    3. The American College of Obstetricians and Gynecologists, *Bleeding During Pregnancy: A Warning Sign* (Washington, D.C., 1985).
    4. Carole Spearin McCauley, *Pregnancy After 35* (New York: E. P. Dutton and Co., Inc., 1976), p. 3.

Chapter 5
    1. Austin H. Kutscher, ed., *But Not to Lose* (New York: Frederick Fall, Inc., 1969), p. 183.

    2. Paul C. MacDonald and Jack A. Pritchard, *Williams Obstetrics, Sixteenth Edition* (New York: Appleton-Century-Crofts, 1980), p. 588.
    3. Ibid., p. 58.
    4. Hank Pizer and Chris Palinski, *Coping With a Miscarriage* (New York: Dial Press, 1980), p. 58.
    5. Ibid., p. 59.
    6. Ibid., p. 61.
    7. Ibid., p. 62.
    8. Ibid., p. 64.
    9. MacDonald and Pritchard, *Williams Obstetrics*, p. 590.
    10. Carole Spearin McCauley, *Pregnancy After 35* (New York: E.P. Dutton and Co., Inc., 1976), p. 47.
    11. Elizabeth Fuller, *Having Your First Baby After 30* (New York: Dodd, Mead and Co., 1983), p. 77.
    12. Carol Ann Rinzler, *The Safe Pregnancy Book* (New York: New American Library, 1984), p. 13.
    13. MacDonald and Pritchard, *Williams Obstetrics*, p. 669.
    14. Ibid., p. 23.
    15. Fuller, *Having Your First Baby*, p. 78.
    16. Lynda Madaras and Jane Patterson, *Womancare* (New York: Avon, 1981), p. 81.
    17. MacDonald and Pritchard, *Williams Obstetrics*, p. 1079.
    18. Ibid., p. 176.
    19. Ibid., p. 2495.
    20. A. Kutscher and Lillian G. Kutscher, eds., *Religion and Bereavement* (New York: Health Sciences Publishing Corp., 1972), p. 60.
    21. Warren W. Wiersbe, *Why Us? When Bad Things Happen to God's People* (Old Tappan, NJ: Fleming Revell, 1984), p. 129.

Chapter 6
    1. A. Kutscher and Lillian G. Kutscher, eds., *Religion and Bereavement* (New York: Health Sciences Publishing Corp., 1972), p. 18.
    2. Nancy Berezin, *After a Loss in Prenancy* (New York: Simon and Schuster, 1982), p. 16.

3. John Langone, *Death Is a Noun* (Boston: Little, Brown, and Co., 1972), p. 108.

4. Linda Madaras and Jane Patterson, *Womancare* (New York: Avon, 1981), p. 12.

5. Elizabeth Fuller, *Having Your First Baby After 35* (New York: Dodd, Mead and Co., 1983), p. 93.

6. Kutscher and Kutscher, *Religion and Bereavement*, p. 280.

7. Ibid., p. 22.

8. Marjorie Holmes, *Hold Me Up a Little Longer, Lord* (New York: Doubleday and Co., Inc., 1977), p. 17.

9. Barbara Berg, *Nothing to Cry About* (New York: Seaview Books, 1981), pp. 116-17.

10. Don Baker, *Pain's Hidden Purpose* (Portland, OR: Multnomah, 1984), p. 73.

Chapter 7

1. A. Kutscher and Lillian G. Kutscher, eds., *Religion and Bereavement* (New York: Health Sciences Publishing Corp., 1972), p. 104.

2. Rana Limbo and Sara Rich Wheeler, "Women's Responses to the Loss of Their Pregnancy Through Miscarriage: A Longitudinal Study" (M.A. thesis, LaCrosse Lutheran Hospital Nursing School, LaCrosse, WI, 1985), p. 2.

3. Maureen Rank, *Free to Grieve* (Minneapolis: Bethany House Publishers, 1985), p. 18.

4. C. S. Lewis, as quoted in *When Hello Means Good-Bye*, Pat Schwiebert and Paul Kirk, (Portland, OR: Perinatal Loss, 1985).

5. Susan Borg and Judith Lasker, *When Pregnancy Fails* (Boston: Beacon Press, 1981), p. 20.

6. Pam Vredevelt, *Empty Arms* (Portland, OR: Multnomah Press, 1984), p. 14.

7. Ann Kiemel Anderson, *Taste of Tears — Touch of God* (Nashville: Oliver Nelson, 1984), p. 85.

8. Nancy Berezin, *After a Loss in Pregnancy* (New York: Simon and Schuster, 1982), p. 16.

9. Joy and Marvin Johnson, *Miscarriage* (Omaha: Centering Corporation, 1983), p. 5.

10. Bernadine Kreis and Alice Pattie, *Up From Grief* (New York: Seabury Press, 1969), p. 22.

Chapter 8

1. Sara Bonnett Stein, *About Dying* (New York: Walker and Co., 1974), p. 10.

2. Bernadine Kreis and Alice Pattie, *Up From Grief* (New York: Seabury Press, 1969), p. 15.

3. Vincent Paris Fish, as quoted in *Religion and Bereavement*, A. Kutscher and Lillian G. Kutscher, eds. (New York: Health Sciences Publishing Corp., 1972), p. 420.

4. Jane Brody, "The New and Often Reassuring Information About Miscarriage," *Redbook* (April 1983), p. 52.

5. Tape by Jack Hayford, "Short-Circuited Into Eternity," #1335 (Van Nuys, CA: Southward Tape Ministry of the Church on the Wave, First Foursquare Church, January 7, 1979).

6. Barbara Berg, *Nothing to Cry About* (New York: Seaview Books, 1981), p. 118.

7. St. Augustine, as quoted in *Religion and Bereavement*, Kutscher and Kutscher, p. 61.

8. Rana Limbo and Sara Rich Wheeler, "Women's Responses to the Loss of Their Pregnancy Through Miscarriage: A Longitudinal Study" (M.A. thesis, LaCrosse Lutheran Hospital Nursing School, LaCrosse, WI, 1985), p. 2.

9. Sherry Lynn Mims Jiminez, *The Other Side of Pregnancy* (Englewood Cliffs, NJ: Prentice-Hall, Inc., 1982), p. 46.

Chapter 9

1. Don Baker, *Pain's Hidden Purpose* (Portland, OR: Multnomah, 1984), p. 89.

2. Ibid., p. 45.

3. Ann Kiemel Anderson, *Taste of Tears — Touch of God* (Nashville: Oliver Nelson, 1984), p. 85.

4. St. Francis de Sales, as quoted in *Religion and Bereavement*, A. Kutscher and Lillian G. Kutscher, eds. (New York: Health Sciences Publishing Corp., 1972), p. 83.

5. Warren Wiersbe, *Why Us? When Bad Things Happen to God's People* (Old Tappan, NJ: Fleming Revell, 1984), p. 84.

6. Jacob Philip Rudin, as quoted in *But Not to Lose*, Austin Kutscher, ed. (New York: Frederick Fell, Inc., 1969), p. 61.

7. Ira J. Tanner, *The Gift of Grief* (New York: Hawthorn Books, 1976), p. 10.

Chapter 10

1. Pam Vredevelt, *Empty Arms* (Portland, OR: Multnomah, 1984), p. 124.

Chapter 11

1. The Compassionate Friends, "Caring for Surviving Children" (Oakbrook, IL, 1982).

2. Marguerita Rudolph, *Should the Children Know?* (New York: Schocken Books, 1978), p. 68.

Chapter 12
1. Rochelle Friedman and Bonnie Gradstein, *Surviving Pregnancy Loss* (Boston: Little, Brown and Co., 1982), p. 35.
2. Ibid.
3. Nancy Berezin, *After a Loss in Pregnancy* (New York: Simon and Schuster, 1982), p. 12.
4. Maureen Rank, *Free to Grieve* (Minneapolis: Bethany House Publishers, 1985), p. 57.
5. Lynda Madaras and Jane Patterson, *Womancare* (New York: Avon, 1981), p. 222.
6. Berezin, *After a Loss*, p. 12.

Chapter 13
1. Hank Pizer and Christine Palinski, *Coping With a Miscarriage* (New York: Dial Press, 1980), p. x.
2. William Shakespeare, as quoted in *Up From Grief*, Bernadine Kreis and Alice Pattie (New York: Seabury Press, 1969), p. 100.
3. Juanita Ryan, *Standing By* (Wheaton, IL: Tyndale House Publishers, 1984), p. 39.
4. Nancy Berezin, *After a Loss in Pregnancy* (New York: Simon and Schuster, 1982), p. 7.
5. Pam Vredevelt, *Empty Arms* (Portland, OR: Multnomah, 1984), p. 41.
6. Joy and Marvin Johnson, *Miscarriage* (Omaha: Centering Corporation, 1983), p. 15.
7. A. Kutscher and Lillian G. Kutscher, eds., *Religion and Bereavement* (New York: Health Sciences Publishing Corp., 1972), p. 101.
8. Ryan, *Standing By*, p. 59.
9. Ibid., p. 62.

Chapter 14
1. Sister Jane Marie Lamb, SHARE Newsletter (Springfield: St. John's Hospital, Summer 1985), p. 9.
2. Sharing Parents, "Sharing Parents: History and Programs" (Sacramento, 1985), p. 1.
3. Lamb, SHARE Newsletter, p. 7.
4. The Compassionate Friends, "When a Child Dies" (Oakbrook, IL, 1985), p. 3.
5. Kinder-Mourn, "When a Child Dies, There Is Help" (Charlotte, N.C.: 1985), p. 4.
6. Karen Anderson, SHARE Newsletter (Springfield: St. John's Hospital, Summer 1985), p. 5.
7. Personal letter from Russell C. Striffler, Director of Chaplaincy, St. Luke's Hospital, Cedar Rapids, Iowa, October 14, 1985.
8. Mothers-Crisis, "Mothers In Crisis" (Joplin, MO: Freeman Hospital, 1985).

Chapter 15
1. Bernadine Kreis and Alice Pattie, *Up From Grief* (New York: Seabury Press, 1969), p. 91.
2. Maureen Rank, *Free to Grieve* (Minneapolis: Bethany House, 1985), p. 139.
3. Dr. James Robinson, as quoted in *Religion and Bereavement*, A. Kutscher and Lillian G. Kutscher, eds. (New York: Health Sciences Publishing Corp., 1972), p. 381.
4. Lynda Madaras and Jane Patterson, *Womancare* (New York: Avon, 1981), p. 30.
5. Hank Pizar and Christine Palinski, *Coping With a Miscarriage* (New York: Dial Press, 1980), p. 190.
6. Walter Trobisch, *A Christian View of Contraception* (Downers Grove, IL: Intervarsity Press), p. 45.
7. Pam Vredevelt, *Empty Arms* (Portland, OR: Multnomah Press, 1984), p. 104.
8. Sherry Lynn Mims Jimenez, *The Other Side of Pregnancy* (Englewood Cliffs, N.J.: Prentice Hall, Inc., 1982), p. 21.
9. Carol Ann Rinzler, *The Safe Pregnancy Book* (New York: New American Library, 1984), p. 82.
10. Ibid.
11. Kathleen Bernau, "Grief and the Loss of Your Baby," (Rose Medical Center, 1984), p. 8.
12. Ann Kiemel Anderson, *Taste of Tears — Touch of God* (Nashville: Oliver Nelson, 1984), p. 201.
13. Trobisch, *A Christian View*, p. 44.

Chapter 16
1. Forward Movement Publications, "Forward Day By Day" (Cincinnati, November 1985-January 1986), p. 9.
2. Forward Movement Publication, "Forward Day By Day" (Cincinnaii, August 1985-October 1985), p. 39.
3. Bernadine Kreis and Alice Pattie, *Up From Grief* (New York: Seabury Press, 1969), p. 170.
4. Warren Wiersbe, *Why Us? When Bad Things Happen to God's People* (Old Tappan, NJ: Fleming Revell, 1984), p. 95.
5. Ibid., p. 115.
6. Forward Movement (August 1985-October 1985), p. 81.